AFRICAN WRITERS SERIES
Founding editor · Chinua Achebe

AFRICAN WRITERS SERIES
127
Nine African Plays for Radio

Nine African Plays
for Radio

edited by
GWYNETH HENDERSON, comp. & ~~COSMO PIETERSE~~

HEINEMANN
LONDON · IBADAN · NAIROBI

Heinemann Educational Books Ltd
48 Charles Street, London WIX 8AH
P.M.B. 5205, Ibadan · P.O. Box 45314, Nairobi
EDINBURGH MELBOURNE TORONTO AUCKLAND
HONG KONG SINGAPORE KUALA LUMPUR NEW DELHI

ISBN 0 435 90127 3

PN
6120
.R2
H395

Printed in Great Britain by
Cox & Wyman Ltd, London, Fakenham and Reading

Contents

Introduction

It is ten years now since the BBC first began producing plays for African Theatre, and so perhaps this collection of plays from the series is overdue. Of course, many of the plays broadcast in African Theatre have been published, but always adapted for the stage rather than as radio plays. Presumably it was thought that plays adapted for the stage would be of more general use to the reader as well as to the potential performer. For the minority who actually wish to mount a production of an individual play, this is true; but for the majority who wish to read it, either individually or in groups, the original radio script has many advantages.

Furthermore, the importance of radio as a medium in Africa, now and in the foreseeable future, although widely recognized, is not reflected in the amount of published material available to those who want to write for it. Very few books or manuals of any description exist to help the uninitiated to understand the different problems and advantages of writing for an audience that is 'blind'. Writing for radio is a specialized technique; but it is no more difficult than writing for any other form of production, and much of the mystique surrounding the technical side needs to be broken down. Later in this introduction there is a short piece about each of the plays in the book, in which any particular problems posed by the script will be discussed. Similarly, there is a glossary of technical terms; these are really surprisingly few.

We hope too that this collection will be of particular value to schools, colleges and anyone who reads plays in groups. They give plenty of scope for experiment with a tape-recorder. Although many of the plays have small casts, members of the class or group can be employed in taking care of sound effects, or being 'crowd'. A child who is too shy to take a speaking part may be very happy to be involved as the sound-effects man who has to make eerie footsteps or slam doors angrily. Sound effects are usually not

difficult to improvise, and can be a good exercise in ingenuity,
even in a professional broadcasting organization. If a tape-recorder
is available for use with the group, this, of course, is ideal; if not,
it is still quite easy to simulate a broadcast by having the
uninvolved members of the group not looking at the actors but
simply listening.

None of this is to say that the plays in this book cannot easily
be performed on the stage. They can. The technical broadcasting
instructions are easily adapted to stage directions with the help of
the glossary.

The only real difference between a stage play and a radio play,
as far as the writer is concerned, is that he must remember all the
time that his audience cannot see what is happening and therefore
needs more help from the dialogue, in order to follow, than it
would if it could see the actors. This means that all the characters
must be not only clearly identified when they make their first
appearance but also re-identified throughout the play. It means
that signposting as to where a scene is taking place must be clear.
It means that the listener must never be in doubt as to what is
happening; once he stops to wonder, he gets lost, and he does not
have his eyes to help him catch up. It means that the number of
characters taking part in a scene must be restricted, since the
listener will get muddled if too many voices are going at once. Of
course, in a radio play the sound effects are by definition
important; but they are not in themselves sufficient to establish
either action or situation. As a general rule, sound effects should
be used only for underlining both action and situation.

All the plays in this book (except *Company Pot*) were originally
intended for production in African Theatre, and so take roughly
thirty minutes to perform; they are consequently all simple in
construction. It is hoped too that this will help to make them
suitable for translation into local languages; this also means that
the situations need to be imaginatively represented in terms which
are familiar to the audience.

Ten years, and nearly one hundred and fifty productions in
African Theatre, inevitably mean that the BBC has broadcast
every type of play by writers from all over Africa. The list of
playwrights reads rather like a *Who's Who* of African writing; it
includes Wole Soyinka, Cyprian Ekwensi, Obi Egbuna, James
Ngugi, Pat Maddy, Mbella Sonne Dipoko, Joe de Graft, Bloke
Modisane, Guillaume Oyono-Mbia, Cameron Duodu, David

Rubadiri, Alfred Hutchinson and many others. Perhaps the only thing these very different writers have in common is that they have written successful radio plays.

The variety of the plays in this book alone proves that in radio, as with any other form of creative writing, any rule can be broken provided that the audience stays with you until the end and goes away without feeling let down or disappointed. Some of these nine plays were less successful in production than I had hoped, some more so. We chose them as being representative of the original plays that have been broadcast over the last two years, not because they are necessarily the best. We both mistrust comparisons of merit.

The order in which the plays are printed here is that in which they were broadcast; on the title page of each, the original cast list appears together with a list of essential sound effects. Where music is necessary we have simply described the type of music used; in none of these plays is a particular song or piece essential. One thing you have to accept very soon as a radio producer is that the right combinations of sound can only be achieved by trial and error; sounds that seem right in isolation, without the action, can sound very different once you put everything together.

It is true that the BBC has a large library of sound-effect records available, but any group that has access to a tape-recorder can start its own. Even without one, it is usually possible to improvise, either with the human voice or with objects that are generally available. For example, in two of the plays gunfire is essential. In the 'African Theatre' production a record was used, but an adequate sound can be achieved (after a bit of practice) by knocking two smallish solid hard objects together very rapidly; this turns the guns into machine guns, which do make a 'rat-tat-tat' rather than the explosive crack of a shotgun or revolver.

These plays, and the characters in them, can be interpreted and performed in many different ways. They will grow and change in reading and rehearsal. We hope you will enjoy reading, acting and producing them as much as we did.

GWYNETH HENDERSON
COSMO PIETERSE

Producer's Notes

Sunil's Dilemma by Kuldip Sondhi

This is the most complicated play in this collection, as far as sound effects, and the placing and movement of the different scenes, are concerned. This makes it less suitable than most for stage production; but it works extremely well as a radio play. The scenes are well balanced in length, and the author makes skilful use of sounds to underline the movement from one room to another. Most of the sound effects can be improvised without much difficulty, with the exception of the car and heavy rain. In fact the rain is not absolutely necessary; use of a sound for thunder – carefully handled so as not to drown the dialogue – would do. The main problem for the producer is to maintain the tension of the play and the ambivalence of the two visitors. The subject-matter of this play, African–Asian relations in an East African country, inevitably gives rise to discussion among the cast. This could lead to problems; but in the production we did, the more we discussed the play at lunch and coffee breaks the better the performances became.

The Soldiers by Robin White

This is one of the plays which every member of the cast liked for the same reasons. In our first discussions in the studio, I was surprised to find that we all had very similar interpretations in mind. The difficult part for everyone was the spacing of climaxes and tension. At one point during rehearsals we went right over the top, and it felt as if all the actors were screaming their lines all the way through. It is an emotionally exhausting play to produce, and to take part in; and this is something that is not always easy to remember. Technically it is straightforward, since it all happens in the same place. The gunfire and a car are the only sound effects that cannot be easily produced. I have already made a suggestion for gunfire; the car arriving and departing could be left out, and the sound of a distant door slamming could be used to underline the dialogue. *The Soldiers* is an example of a written

construction which works very well as a radio play. The first few
lines establish the setting, the atmosphere and the theme clearly
and quickly; there is plenty of action to keep the listener's
interest; and although there are climaxes and moments of tension
all the way through, these are spaced out and leave something
in reserve for the final explosion; which, although inevitable, is
still shocking and surprising. The characters are clearly defined
and identified, not only by name but also through the different
way in which each one speaks. The two soldiers differ widely in
their use of language. Because *The Soldiers* is technically simple,
and the characterization straightforward, I thought it would be an
easy play to produce; it was not, because of its subject-matter.
But it worked.

The Trial of Busumbala by Gabriel Roberts
After reading this play twice I was still unsure about it. It has
some excellent characterization, some hilarious dialogue, and
plenty of surprises; and yet whether or not the punch at the end
comes off depends very much on the listener or reader. If *The
Trial of Busumbala* has a weakness, this is it, but its merits more
than compensate. As a play to take part in, to produce, or just to
hear, it is enormous fun. Technically it is straightforward, and
would be as easy to perform on stage as it is for radio. All the
sound effects can be produced in an ordinary room without
special equipment. The essence of a successful production of the
play is in the casting of the characters. In this, more than in any
other play in the collection, the pomposity of one character, the
pig-headedness of another, and the idiocy of yet another, must be
immediately apparent in the way they speak; otherwise a great
deal of the vitality and farcical quality of the play will be lost.

The Prisoner, the Judge and the Jailer by Derlene Clems
Although the sound effects for this play seemed, on first reading,
to be the most complicated part of the producer's job, in fact the
biggest problem turned out to be the pacing of the acting. The
suspense was difficult to maintain. In this, more perhaps than in
any other play in the collection, we had to spend quite a large
proportion of rehearsal time discussing where the climaxes are and
where the mood changes. To keep an audience's interest variations
in pace, intensity and mood are essential. Technically, the almost
constant sound of rain may seem to be an insuperable problem

without the aid of a recording; but in fact the script is so explicit in its references to the rain and the setting of the action that the actual sound is not a necessity. The thunder can be dispensed with, as can the passing lorry. *The Prisoner, the Judge and the Jailer* is a good example of a play in which the writing creates the atmosphere so successfully that sound effects are really unimportant. It would also transfer easily, to a stage production for the same reason. This is a good example of how to use sound effects in writing for radio: they serve to underline the action or the setting, but never to establish them on their own.

Oh, how dearly I detest thee by Jeanne Ngo Libondo
This play seems to fly in the face of many of the obvious requirements of a successful radio play; in particular, the long monologue at the end is an obvious strain on the listener's patience, and throws the structure out of balance. And yet the play does come off in performance – although nobody should take its construction as a model! As it was, even with such a good and experienced actress as Jumoke Debayo in the part, she and I found ourselves pruning the speech during rehearsals. The variations in pace that this play achieves – and its mixture of comedy and tragedy – make it interesting to produce. Again, this is straightforward technically. There are plenty of sound effects, but all of them can be made in an ordinary room without any special equipment.

Lagos, Yes, Lagos by Yemi Ajibade
This again is an enjoyable play to produce and take part in. This is partly because the baddies win and there is no hint of a moral anywhere, but mainly because of the tremendous good humour which emanates from the characters and the play.

It has a comparatively large cast for a half-hour play, but the characters are well and skilfully defined, so that there is no danger of a listener getting muddled. One of the scenes takes place in a market; in our production we used a record for the general atmosphere, but the cast joined in as well to give the right depth. There are no other effects that cannot be easily come by, or easily improvised.

Beyond the Line by Laban Erapu
On first reading, this appears to break a golden rule of

construction; nothing happens at all until three-quarters of the way through, and then there is a lot of action for the last quarter. But in *Beyond the Line* the quality of the dialogue, and the variations in pace and intensity, more than justify the risks the author took. The subject-matter makes for lots of rehearsal discussion, and time has to be allowed for this. However, once we had discussed the subject and the characters in the play, the production was one of the easiest I have ever done, because after we had reached agreement it directed itself as far as pace and intensity were concerned. Technically, there are no effects that cannot be produced in any ordinary room.

Full-Cycle by Gordon Tialobi

The cast are still arguing about the equivocal ending of *Full-Cycle*, and the author still refuses to comment on the different theories. But it is not only the ending that provides difficulties for the producer. The tension and the weird zaniness of the whole play can be difficult, first to build up, and then to restrain. It is a play which can make both producer and actors feel inadequate, simply because it demands so much from both. Technically the most difficult problem is to maintain the speed and sharpness of both the voices and the sound effects without the final product being at a constant high pitch. The audience needs to be given some relief. All this means that I found this a difficult play to produce; but it also means that everyone involved cared about the result, because we thought that what the plays says is important. There are certain sound effects that are essential for *Full-Cycle* – an alarm clock, drum beats, gong beats and gunfire – but all can fairly easily be improvised.

Company Pot by Patience Henaku Addo

This is the only play in the collection which was not specially written for radio but adapted for us by the author. Admittedly, I was concerned as to whether the speeches directed to the audience would come off, but in the event they certainly did. The conventions of the Ghanaian concert-party style transferred perfectly to radio, with very little help from the producer. The help needed was in making sure that, for example with the speeches to the audience, the actresses changed their tone and their approach. At the end of the play music was used to punctuate Akyebi's last speech at the moment when she turns to the audience to deliver her epilogue. This is another play which exudes jollity. Technically it is simple, the only essential sound effects being an alarm clock and music. The music can be chosen to fit the national context; and, of course, it would be simple to change the place names for the same reason.

GWYNETH HENDERSON

Glossary of Technical Terms

FADE The mechanism used to control the volume of voices and sound effects (whether on record or tape) is a type of knob which can be turned quickly or slowly so the producer can bring in and up the combinations of sound (or take them down and out) to suit the mood and action of the scene.

FX Simply shorthand for sound effects like doors opening or closing. It covers all sound effects, whether done in the studio, on record or on tape. In a professional radio production the script would probably also differentiate between sound effects to be made by tape and disc recordings, and to be done in the studio. Those done in the studio are called 'spot effects'.

MIC Microphone. Where the actors, or sound-effects man, stand in relation to the microphone governs the perspectives and the movement that the listener hears. For example, if the action demands that a character enters a room through a door, the door and the actor must sound as if they are in the same place. Then to bring the actor into the centre of the room he must move up to the microphone while he is speaking so that the audience hears him move. Therefore in a script the directions are 'coming on mic'.

PEAK Bringing up background sound effects in the middle of a scene, holding them at full strength and then fading under the actors' voices. This is a useful technique in scenes like the market scene in *Lagos, Yes, Lagos* where the action shifts from one group of characters to another in the same setting at the same time.

Sunil's Dilemma

KULDIP SONDHI

Kuldip Sondhi, *born in Lahore in 1924, was educated in Kenya before gaining an M.Sc. in aeronautical engineering in the U.S.A. Three of his other plays have been published,* Undesignated *in* Short East African Plays *and* Encounter *in* Ten One-Act Plays *as well as* The Magic Pool *in* Short African Plays (*Heinemann Educational Books*). Sunil's Dilemma *was the fifth of his plays to be broadcast by the BBC in* African Theatre.

Recorded Sunday 12th April 1970

CAST
Sunil – Renu Satna
Kamau – Abdi Abubakar
Rashid – Bloke Modisane
Devi – Usha Joshi
SOUND EFFECTS
Rain
Thunder
Door with lock
Light switch
Crockery
Glasses
Bottle
Car revving
Car doors
Car departing
Metal tools
Keys

Place: Sunil's bungalow on the outskirts of Nairobi
Time: The present, late one night

fx: Sound of doors being locked. Thunder in distance

DEVI: Are all the doors locked, Sunil?

SUNIL: Yes.

DEVI: And the windows?

SUNIL: I'm shutting them.

DEVI: You've left the garage light on.

SUNIL: It's a good advertisement.

DEVI: It's also a temptation.

SUNIL: Who would want to steal tools and some spare parts?

DEVI: I wish we lived in the centre of Nairobi, in an upstairs flat, surrounded by people.

SUNIL: Oh no!

DEVI: We're right on the edge of the city here, Sunil, next to the game park. It's almost like living in the bush.

SUNIL: But it's beautiful, Devi. There aren't many places in the world like it.

DEVI: I'm sure there aren't!

SUNIL: Oh, all right, never satisfied, always moaning about your fate. You're ungrateful, that's what you are, ungrateful for what we have!

DEVI: I'm afraid, Sunil, not ungrateful.

SUNIL: Oh, for heaven's sake! What's there to be afraid of, a few wild animals? We're not tourists!

DEVI: This isn't a safe country for us, Sunil. We're not wanted here and you know it. The Africans say so every day. Do you deny it?

SUNIL: There you go again.

DEVI: Well, it's a fact isn't it? Look how many Asians have left for other parts of the world.

SUNIL: That's their business. Whatever our difficulties, this is where we belong. Accept that once and for all, and get close to the people. Get close to the people, Devi.

DEVI: I wish you wouldn't talk to me like a politician.

SUNIL: But I only meant . . .

DEVI: I know what you meant. It's not the first time that you've told me to get close to the people.

SUNIL: Well, then, why don't you?

DEVI: I don't know. There doesn't seem to be much hope for us here . . . (*Yawns*) I'm so tired these days . . . that's half my trouble.

SUNIL: It's the thundery weather. You'll feel better when it starts raining.

DEVI: I hope so. (*Going off mic*) I'm going to bed. Check the doors and windows again, Sunil.

SUNIL: Don't worry, go to bed now. You're just tired.

Fade out

Fade in

fx: Thunder. Sound of rain. Sound of knocking – grows louder

DEVI: (*Whispers*) Sunil . . . Sunil!

SUNIL: (*Sleepily*) Uh, what's the matter?

DEVI: Someone's outside.

SUNIL: It's the rain, Devi, go to sleep.

DEVI: No, listen carefully, there is someone.

SUNIL: Go to sleep for heaven's sake . . .

fx: Knocking heard in rain. Bed creaks

DEVI: (*Going off mic*) Let me find out, it might be an open window. (*Muffled scream*)

SUNIL: (*Awakening*) What's . . . happening?

DEVI: (*Coming in on mic quickly*) There are two Africans at the window, Sunil – two Africans!

SUNIL: You're dreaming!

DEVI: I saw them, I tell you – two Africans in black raincoats and one of them waved to me.

fx: Sound of knocking

There, hear it!

SUNIL: Yes. Someone's there.

DEVI: I'll phone the police.

SUNIL: No. Let me see them first. You can't tell about Africans these days, might be some big Government people, anybody. (*Going off mic*) We don't want to offend them.

fx: Sound of knocking

DEVI: (*Whispers*) There they are in the porch – behind the window!

SUNIL: Yes. Well, I'll just open the window and talk to them.

fx: Open window creaks – peak rain sharply

(*Loudly*) What is it, who are you?

KAMAU: (*Shouts from off mic*) We are the police, sir. From the Secret Branch.

RASHID: (*Shouts from off mic*) Let us in bwana.

SUNIL: What for?

RASHID: We need help.

KAMAU: Our car is broken down, sir. Isn't that your garage?

SUNIL: It is.

DEVI: (*Whispers*) I don't trust them, Sunil!

SUNIL: Do you have any identification on you?

KAMAU: We do. I am Inspector Kamau. Here is my card. And this is Constable Rashid. Hold it up constable. Can you see it sir?

DEVI: (*Whispers*) It's a trick!

SUNIL: (*Whispers*) Please, don't make things more difficult than they are.

DEVI: But they're complete strangers to us!

fx: Noise of window shutting

SUNIL: That's why we must help them. Imagine if I was kept waiting outside like this?

DEVI: But . . .

SUNIL: Now stop worrying. (*Going off mic*) I'll go out and talk to them. They don't look like ruffians to me.

Fade out

fx: Door unlocks and opens. Bring up rain sharply

SUNIL: Well, what's all this about?

KAMAU: A robbery took place at the other end of the city earlier on in the evening, sir. The police have spread out in every direction, some in uniform and some in plain clothes. The criminals could be anywhere. We are playing them at their own game and going after them in an ordinary civilian car. Do you see the point, sir?

SUNIL: I do, but you don't expect me to go out in the rain to repair your car do you?

KAMAU: No, but when it stops for a few minutes could you look at it?

SUNIL: I suppose so. Anyhow, you'd better come in for a while. I don't see any sign of the rain stopping just yet.

fx: Door shuts – cut rain

This is my wife.

KAMAU: How do you do, madam.

DEVI: How do you do.

KAMAU: We are very sorry to disturb you so late, madam.

DEVI: It can't be helped. My husband will help you if he can.

KAMAU: Thank you. You are being very kind to us.

SUNIL: Not at all. We must help one another. Devi, do you think we could have some tea while we wait for the rain to stop?

DEVI: (*Going off mic*) Yes. I'll make some.

RASHID: So many things – look at that big refrigerator!

SUNIL: What? (*Laughing*) Oh yes, the house is rather full up. But come on and sit down in the living-room. It's more comfortable in there.

RASHID: You have everything!

SUNIL: I wish I did! Actually a lot of the things in this house have been picked up in auctions. That refrigerator you saw in the dining-room, for instance, was fit for the scrap yard before I did it up. I am a mechanic after all.

KAMAU: Also a successful businessman from what I can see.

RASHID: What Asian is not a businessman?

KAMAU: Well, this one is ready to share his happiness with us. Am I right sir?

SUNIL: You're in my house aren't you?

KAMAU: Quite right, sir. (*Both laugh*)

SUNIL: Won't you sit down, inspector?

KAMAU: Thank you. Ah, this is a comfortable room.

RASHID: (*Going off mic*) I want to see what's in that refrigerator . . .

KAMAU: Ask before you touch anything, bwana Rashid.

RASHID: (*Calls from off mic*) What is there to ask?

KAMAU: Careful, constable!

fx: Door shuts

SUNIL: These robbers you're after, inspector . . .

KAMAU: Yes?

SUNIL: Are they dangerous?

KAMAU: Could be. Like snakes, they can all bite. Some kill, others merely frighten and some simply pass you by.

SUNIL: In other words, always be ready for the worst?

KAMAU: Quite.

SUNIL: Well, I wish you luck.

KAMAU: Thank you. Luck is what we do need tonight. All of us do.

SUNIL: (*Laughs*) Er . . . yes. I suppose you are right.

fx: Door opens

RASHID: (*Coming in on mic*) That refrigerator is like a shop, bwana Kamau. It's full of things!

KAMAU: Food is the important thing for constable Rashid.

RASHID: His wife could warm some of it for us. I would like some eggs.

KAMAU: The bwana's wife will refuse to give us anything if she hears you talking like that.

RASHID: I have never received anything from the hands of an Asian woman.

KAMAU: Say you are hungry, constable, and leave it at that – actually we have been on the move for many hours, sir.

SUNIL: Well, let him take a beer from the fridge. I'll fetch glasses from the kitchen and ask Devi to cook some food.

KAMAU: Thank you. Can I help?

SUNIL: (*Going off mic*) No, that's all right, inspector. Stay here. I won't be a minute.

fx: Door shuts

RASHID: They've certainly got more than enough for two here!

KAMAU: He's probably worked hard for it.

RASHID: The usual Asian success story, huh?

fx: Door opens

SUNIL: (*Coming in on mic*) Here's your glass, constable.

RASHID: Ah, good.

SUNIL: A beer for you too, inspector?

KAMAU: Yes, thank you. Strictly speaking one doesn't drink on duty, but this is an exception.

SUNIL: I won't tell anyone.

KAMAU: (*Laughs*) No, I don't think you will.

RASHID: Is she making some food for us?

SUNIL: Yes. Look, constable, if you are that hungry go to the fridge in the dining room and help yourself till the eggs are ready.

RASHID: (*Going off mic*) Good. I'll do that.

fx: Door closes

KAMAU: Aren't you having some beer, sir?

SUNIL: No, I'll wait for the tea, inspector. I don't normally drink at this hour.

KAMAU: (*Laughs*) Nor do I, normally. (*Pause*) What a fine lady your wife is, sir.

SUNIL: Nice of you to say so.

KAMAU: I'm so happy you introduced me to her.

SUNIL: The truth is you have proved to be a pleasant surprise.

KAMAU: Did she say that?

SUNIL: Yes.

KAMAU: A charming person, if I may say so.

SUNIL: She is very co-operative really.

KAMAU: You are lucky.

SUNIL: Why?

KAMAU: To have a wife who always obeys you.

SUNIL: Oh we do have our differences.

KAMAU: Naturally.

fx: Door opens suddenly

RASHID: (*Calls from off mic*) Do not forget me, bwana Kamau.

KAMAU: I am not far from you, constable. The bwana and I are having a friendly talk.

RASHID: (*Off mic*) Ah, a friendly talk! (*Mutters to himself*) It always begins with a friendly talk. (*Loud*) I am opening another bottle. This waiting makes me thirsty.

fx: Door shuts

SUNIL: (*Laughs*) Really!

KAMAU: Do not ignore him, bwana. That would be a mistake.

SUNIL: Well, I've told him to help himself from the fridge. (*Whispers*) But I believe my wife fears him.

KAMAU: Most women do, and he knows it. That's why I encourage his appetite for food. Keeps him occupied.

SUNIL: Let him eat as much as he wants to. What about yourself?

KAMAU: Food doesn't interest me much. I have other needs.

SUNIL: Not like him, eh?

KAMAU: I hope not! Did your wife notice the difference between us?

SUNIL: Doesn't think of you as an African at all.

KAMAU: Really?

SUNIL: Not at all.

KAMAU: What does she take me to be?

SUNIL: Oh, she knows you are an African, of course, but your race no longer means anything to her. That's what I mean really. And it's a healthy sign, mark you.

KAMAU: Well, she is a healthy woman, and before we part I'm going to express my gratitude to her.

SUNIL: She'll appreciate that.

KAMAU: Not as an African to an Asian.

SUNIL: Of course not.

KAMAU: But as a man to a woman.

SUNIL: That's the only reasonable way.

KAMAU: She should know how I feel about her kindness.

SUNIL: You're welcome in this house, inspector.

KAMAU: I'm beginning to feel very much at home.

fx: Door opens

RASHID: (*Calling from off mic*) Bwana Kamau!

KAMAU: Yes?

RASHID: Why not warn him that marriages do not last?

KAMAU: Yes, yes, all right! Is it still raining?

RASHID: It is. We may be here for some time.

KAMAU: You have been allowed to take what you want from the refrigerator, constable.

RASHID: Hot food would be better.

SUNIL: It's being prepared. (*Low*) Funny man!

KAMAU: Not always funny, but I have to put up with him.

SUNIL: Yes, so I see. Are you married yourself, inspector?

KAMAU: Married and parted.

SUNIL: I'm sorry to hear that.

KAMAU: No, it's not surprising. I always do what I want to, and that doesn't work in marriage.

SUNIL: How right you are!

KAMAU: You have problems too?

SUNIL: Yes! You see, well no, it's stupid, how can I discuss it with you?

KAMAU: Do you think I wouldn't understand?

SUNIL: Oh, I'm sure you would, but I don't think we know each other well enough.

KAMAU: As you please.

SUNIL: (*Moving off mic*) Let me show you the rest of the house, inspector.

KAMAU: (*Moving off mic*) Yes, I'd like to see it.

SUNIL: We can go out through this door.

fx: Door opens – two sets of footsteps

SUNIL: The bedrooms are off this corridor.

KAMAU: I see.

SUNIL: And there's a yard down the end at the back. It's a large plot. If we stayed on in this country the house could be extended in that direction.

KAMAU: Are you thinking of leaving?

SUNIL: That's the problem.

KAMAU: The problem you didn't want to discuss?

SUNIL: Well, it's connected with it. (*Pause*) Women are never satisfied, you know, Mr Kamau.

KAMAU: I know. And when they are it's not for long.

SUNIL: How right you are! Anyhow let me not burden you with my domestic problems. (*Pause*) Well, you see she comes from a family of educated people. My wife is related to lawyers, engineers and doctors, while I . . . I am just a mechanic. I have had some success in business too, as you guessed, but no matter how successful I become I can never be more than a worker in her eyes. Just an ordinary worker.

KAMAU: (*Laughs softly*)

SUNIL: You don't believe me?

KAMAU: I don't disbelieve you, but is that really the whole story?

SUNIL: Yes. I can't think of any other reason.

KAMAU: In my experience women lie a lot.

SUNIL: But in my case, I mean, well, in my case it's straightforward.

KAMAU: The way she lies?

SUNIL: You make it sound ridiculous.

KAMAU: Do I?

SUNIL: Well . . .

KAMAU: My friend, the real problem is, how does she lie under you?

SUNIL: What?

KAMAU: Yes.

SUNIL: Well . . . er . . . I'm more inclined that way than she is. Yes, I am.

KAMAU: Are you quite sure?

SUNIL: No, not really.

KAMAU: Hey, what's happened?

SUNIL: Damn! The lights have failed.

KAMAU: It's dark everywhere.

SUNIL: The fuse must have gone. Sorry about this, but it'll soon be put right. The fuse-box is quite close to where we're standing.

fx: Sound of movement in corridor. Door closes quietly while Sunil, intent on his own movements, continues talking, not knowing that Kamau has left

Wish I had some kind of light, I'm feeling my way along the wall, Mr Kamau, and you do the same. When you touch something it will be the fuse-box. (*Giggles*) I hope! Funny thing, Mr Kamau, we've just met and I feel that we already know each other so well, funny, isn't it? (*Laughs quietly*) There's some truth in what you say about my wife. (*Sighs*) I've made money but she wants prestige and a social position with it. (*Pause*) Bwana Kamau, why are you so quiet? Not a word from you! (*Coughs – silence*) This fuse will be put right in a few minutes. (*Stumbles*) Damn, I can't see a thing. (*Hoarse whisper*) Bwana Kamau, for God's sake answer: where are you?

fx: Creak of door opening

Ah, I should have guessed. You went out for a light didn't you . . . (*Giggles*) . . . to bring light and happiness into my life, not like that thick friend of yours . . . (*Sound of heavy breathing drawing closer*) You sound out of breath, inspector, what's the matter . . . (*Gasps as Rashid grabs him by the throat*)

RASHID: Playing tricks, are you?

SUNIL: (*Choking*) Let go, damn you.

RASHID: Put the light on.

SUNIL: Let go . . . (*Fit of coughing*) . . . You're mad – ugh!

RASHID: Talk politely to me, you Asian, now put the lights on!

SUNIL: That's what I'm trying to do.

RASHID: You did it on purpose.

SUNIL: Don't be so stupid – ugh – sorry, bwana . . . let go, for God's sake.

RASHID: From the moment we met I've seen the contempt in your eyes – you think I'm good for nothing, don't you – answer me, you Asian!

SUNIL: (*Choked voice*) For heaven's sake, man, let me put the lights on!

RASHID: (*Letting go*) All right. Be quick about it.

SUNIL: (*Coughing*) How can I be quick about it when I can't see a damn thing? Where's Mr Kamau?

RASHID: In the kitchen.

SUNIL: Kitchen – how did he get there?

RASHID: It's not dark in the kitchen.

SUNIL: What? Ah, yes, of course, I quite forgot. The kitchen's on a different fuse. God, what a mess! (*Pause*) Would you let me pass, constable.

RASHID: You should be tried by a court and locked up.

SUNIL: For what?

RASHID: For laughing at me. And if you ever mock me again you know what I'll do – now go!

fx: Fade. Sound of crockery and cooking

SUNIL: Didn't you know that all the lights went out, Devi?

DEVI: No, I'm sorry, Sunil. The door was shut. I heard and saw nothing.

KAMAU: It's my fault. I came in here and got talking to your wife and forgot all about you.

SUNIL: I wish you hadn't.

KAMAU: Why, what's happened?

SUNIL: Tell you later. Give me a box of matches, Devi.

DEVI: Shall I come along, Sunil?

SUNIL: No, you remain here and finish your cooking. The inspector can help me with the fuse.

DEVI: I'll keep a plate warm for you, inspector.
KAMAU: Thank you. It's very kind of you.

fx: Door opens and closes. Cut crockery noises

SUNIL: Where's that constable?
KAMAU: Not here. Must be in the living-room.
SUNIL: Well, he just assaulted me, for your information.
KAMAU: What?
SUNIL: Yes! No reason at all. Just came for me like a madman.
KAMAU: (*Sighs*) He's a bad case. But leave it to me, I'll deal with
   him later.
SUNIL: Personally I doubt if he's right in the head. Try the
   switch now.

fx: Click of light switch

KAMAU: Ah, lights at last.
SUNIL: I'm seriously thinking of putting in a complaint to the
   police, in writing.
KAMAU: Just try and forget what happened, bwana mechanic.
   That man has many burdens in life. That is why he eats and
   drinks so much. He doesn't know what to do with himself.
SUNIL: I hope he chokes, the bastard.
KAMAU. You have every right to be angry, of course. Shall we
   return to the kitchen now. Your wife's waiting.

Fade out

Fade in

fx: Sounds of crockery and eating

KAMAU: An excellent omelette, madam, I enjoyed it very much.

DEVI: There's more if you like.
KAMAU: I'd like to take some for the constable if you don't mind.
SUNIL: Why do you take such creatures into the police?
KAMAU: It's difficult to judge people in advance.
SUNIL: Anyone can see the difference between you two.
DEVI: There's no comparison – is that enough?
KAMAU: (*Laughing*) If it isn't, then he deserves to go hungry.
   Thank you. (*Going off mic*) I'll take it to him.

fx: Door opens and closes

DEVI: What a nice man.

SUNIL: You're becoming very friendly with that African.

DEVI: Didn't you tell me to get friendly with these people?

SUNIL: There are limits.

DEVI: I haven't crossed them.

SUNIL: You go from one extreme to another.

DEVI: Always grumbling at me, anything I do is wrong.

SUNIL: I didn't say it's wrong, but you're restless. You're not behaving gracefully.

DEVI: I've done nothing that you need be ashamed of.

SUNIL: What does that mean?

DEVI: I don't know what you suspect, but it's not true.

SUNIL: And what do I suspect?

DEVI: Please don't carry on like this.

SUNIL: What did you two talk about?

DEVI: Mr Kamau told me how much he admires this house and your success.

SUNIL: What does Mr Kamau know about me or my success? This is the first time we've met.

DEVI: He's travelled all over the world, Sunil. He understands a lot, that man.

SUNIL: I'm sure he does.

DEVI: He has ambitions, Sunil.

SUNIL: In what?

DEVI: Oh, in everything. He wants to get ahead in life, he told me. In my opinion this is the sort of African we should take into partnership.

SUNIL: What about your plans for getting away from here and from these people?

DEVI: I'm always ready.

SUNIL: Are you?

DEVI: Of course. You know that.

SUNIL: I'm wondering how well I do know you.

DEVI: What do you want me to do, Sunil? Please tell me that instead of making all these funny remarks.

SUNIL: I don't want you to do anything, Devi. Just go to bed after this. Leave everything to me now. I'm going to find out a little more about him. Do you hear?

DEVI: Yes, Sunil.

fx: Door opens and shuts – Sunil's footsteps

B

SUNIL: Oh, you're alone, constable?

RASHID: Yes.

SUNIL: Did you get enough food?

RASHID: Yes I did. Thank you.

SUNIL: Where's bwana Kamau?

RASHID: Gone to the lavatory.

SUNIL: Ah. (*Pause*) How do you feel now?

RASHID: About what?

SUNIL: About things in general.

RASHID: What's it to you?

SUNIL: Nothing. I just wondered.

RASHID: Well, I feel a little better.

SUNIL: What's your trouble?

Pause

RASHID: No-one likes me.

SUNIL: How can you say that?

RASHID: Because it's the truth.

SUNIL: Oh, come now! What about your family?

RASHID: My family?

SUNIL: Yes. Your wife, your children. They love you – don't they?

RASHID: My wife ran away.

SUNIL: Oh. Anyhow, she'll probably return after a while. They often do. Women can be like that. Happy today, unhappy tomorrow, then happy again. Don't you agree?

RASHID: No. (*Pause*) My wife is an educated woman. She was never happy with me.

SUNIL: I'm sorry for you.

RASHID: Why?

SUNIL: I don't know. There's no reason for it.

RASHID: You're not as bad as I thought. (*Pause*) Listen!

SUNIL: Yes?

RASHID: Be careful of bwana Kamau.

SUNIL: Why . . . isn't he your friend?

RASHID: Kamau took my wife.

SUNIL: Ah. So that's it.

RASHID: Yes.

SUNIL: And now she lives with him?

RASHID: No.

SUNIL: Then she left him too?

RASHID: No. He left her.

SUNIL: Oh . . . oh, I see. But then she's sure to return to you.

RASHID: (*Bitter chuckle*) No. She walks the streets of Nairobi now. Anyone can get her. Anyone but me.

SUNIL: My God, you do have troubles. I'm sure she'll realize her mistake soon. I think that one of these days she'll return to you and ask for forgiveness.

RASHID: No. Not her. What do I have to offer? (*Pause*) But if I made money, that would make a difference. Money would make a difference. Then she might return.

SUNIL: There you see, there is hope!

fx: Cough in distance

RASHID: That's Kamau. Don't discuss any of this in front of him.

SUNIL: No, I won't.

fx: Door shuts off mic in distance

RASHID: Must have gone out to see the car.

SUNIL: Yes. (*Pause*) You know, I think you should start your own life away from him. He's too much for you. You will never amount to anything as long as you stay close to the inspector.

RASHID: I have to.

SUNIL: But why?

RASHID: Because I . . . I am nothing on my own. I don't know how to do anything well. I have no learning, no fine manners. I . . . I . . . (*Bringing it out*) You know my wife called me an animal when she left. I beat her but it made no difference. She said it only proved what she thought of me. And she was right! But if you had met her, you would never believe any of the things I've told you about her! She dresses so well, she speaks so well, very much like bwana Kamau in that respect. (*Strangled voice*) I should kill them both, but if I do I'll have nothing left in this world, nothing. And yet we were so happy together when he first came. I was a constable in those days.

SUNIL: Was?

RASHID: What?

SUNIL: Nothing. Carry on please.

RASHID: I've told you enough. Any beer left?

SUNIL: No. But would you like to try some of this whisky instead?

RASHID: Yes, I would. Give me the bottle.
SUNIL: Here you are, bwana constable.
RASHID: Don't be too sure.
SUNIL: About what?
RASHID: About anything.
SUNIL: I have my doubts about a few things.
RASHID: That's sensible.

fx: Drink poured out

Keep an eye on her.
SUNIL: On who?
RASHID: She has a healthy body and a good laugh.
SUNIL: Who?
RASHID: Your wife.
SUNIL: What?
RASHID: You don't believe me?
SUNIL: Well . . . er . . . we are brought up differently.
RASHID: When she wants to nothing will stop her. They are all the same in that. I'll have another drink.

fx: Drink poured out

My God, I wish I could forget it!
SUNIL: You should!
RASHID: Yes, I should. But how can I forget – Kamau and her together.
SUNIL: Kamau was in the police force in those days?
RASHID: Yes.
SUNIL: As an inspector?
RASHID: What?
SUNIL: Oh, I just wondered if it was due to his position that your wife fell for him.
RASHID: Why, don't you understand the kind of man he is? Since that affair there have been others in his life. And it is always someone else's wife. He specializes in them.
SUNIL: One of these days your friend will get into serious trouble. (*Pause*) But tell me, bwana, who are you really after tonight?
RASHID: Some thieves.
SUNIL: You hope to catch them?
RASHID: We must. They got away with a lot of money. Why are you putting that bottle away?

SUNIL: You've had enough.

RASHID: Don't talk to me like that – give me the bottle!

SUNIL: For heaven's sake – here! You drink a lot for a policeman.

RASHID: Call me Mzee in future.

SUNIL: Why – you're not an old man.

RASHID: You know that Mzee is as much a word of respect as of old age.

SUNIL: I'm ready to give you your due, but anything more would be a lie.

RASHID: You're an Asian, aren't you?

SUNIL: Of course.

RASHID: Then you must be a liar!

SUNIL: I'm tired of your insults. You've been abusing my hospitality from the moment you stepped into this house – my house!

RASHID: My country!

SUNIL: Well then, I'll leave your damned country.

RASHID: You could be deported for that.

KAMAU: (*Coming in on mic*) Hello, what's happening?

RASHID: He has insulted us. The whole country has been dragged into the mud by this Asian.

SUNIL: It isn't me who dragged your wife into the mud.

KAMAU: What kind of talk is this?

RASHID: I'll throttle him!

KAMAU: Go and wait for me in the car.

RASHID: But . . .

KAMAU: Go, man! We'll soon be leaving.

RASHID: (*Going off mic*) I could kill you all!

fx: Door slams

KAMAU: What happened?

SUNIL: His head's full of amazing stories. He suspects every one of something or the other.

KAMAU: I warned you about him. Did he say that I stole his wife?

SUNIL: Yes.

KAMAU: I'm not surprised. He thinks everyone is after her, particularly me.

SUNIL: Then she has run away?

KAMAU: Of course. You've seen the kind of man he is. Anyhow, time we were on our way. It's stopped raining.

SUNIL: Yes, let's go and have a look at that car of yours – we'll
    have to push it to the garage.
KAMAU: Oh well, it's not far. Will it be possible for me to thank
    your wife before we leave?
SUNIL: She's gone to bed.
KAMAU: I would not want her to think badly of us, bwana.
SUNIL: She forms her own opinions.
KAMAU: I'm sure she does. Your wife was such a wonderful
    surprise to me.
SUNIL: Was she?
KAMAU: Oh yes! Her thoughts are clear, her laugh so pleasant.
SUNIL: Her laugh eh?
KAMAU: To hear it is to forget all your troubles.
SUNIL: Maybe I don't make her laugh enough.
KAMAU: (*Laughs*) Maybe.

Fade out

Fade in

RASHID: Here, at last!
SUNIL: Yes, it was further than we thought.

fx: Keys jangle – garage door unlocks and opens

    Right, let's have the bonnet up. There!
RASHID: Now, get going, you Asian.
KAMAU: Constable! It would have to rain again. My shoes and
    trousers are soaked.
RASHID: So are mine. Do you keep any drinks in here, bwana
    mechanic?
SUNIL: This is a garage, not a bar.
RASHID: I wish I had brought some of that food with me. Or the
    whisky. There's half a bottle left on the dining-room table.
    (*Pause*) Can he go and bring something to warm us all,
    bwana? (*Pause*) It was hard work.
SUNIL: (*Silence*) All right, I don't mind.
KAMAU: Thank you, bwana, that's kind.
SUNIL: But be quick about it. If this repair turns out to be no
    more than a block in the fuel line, it won't take long.
KAMAU: (*Going off mic*) I'll be back in a few minutes.

SUNIL: (*Shouts after him*) Knock and announce yourself, or my wife will be frightened.

KAMAU: Not of me, brother! (*Laughs*)

fx: Car starter activated. Car doesn't start

SUNIL: Pass me the three-eighths inch spanner, yes, that small one there, there in front of your eyes – thank you!

RASHID: What are you so angry about?

SUNIL: I don't want to discuss it!

RASHID: Everything I say and do is wrong – is that it?

SUNIL: Everything you've said and done to me is wrong, yes, it is wrong – and stupid!

RASHID: I may have been stupid in the past but it seems you are no cleverer.

SUNIL: What do you mean by that?

RASHID: Well, how can you allow him to visit your wife alone?

SUNIL: He's not visiting her! He's just gone there to get something.

RASHID: (*Chuckles coarsely*) Yes, he has.

SUNIL: What are you getting at?

RASHID: Do I have to say it?

SUNIL: Do you want this bloody car repaired or not?

RASHID: I do.

SUNIL: Well then, talk less and work more.

RASHID: To work, bwana!

SUNIL: High time you two were on your way. Nothing but insults all the time.

RASHID: I was giving you good advice.

SUNIL: I don't need your advice – pass me that screwdriver.

RASHID: He's ruthless. Doesn't care for anyone but himself. That's his method.

SUNIL: Screwdriver please!

RASHID: Yes, bwana!

SUNIL: Damn these nuts!

RASHID: At first we were so happy. Then his eyes fell on my wife and nothing could stop him.

SUNIL: Hardly sounds human, the way you carry on about that man.

RASHID: I saw him in action once.

SUNIL: There, it's off at last.

RASHID: It was terrible.

SUNIL: The nuts are rusted through and through.

RASHID: I thought the woman had been bewitched.

SUNIL: And the butterfly valve's stuck in the carburettor. That's the real trouble.

RASHID: She just made herself available to him.

SUNIL: You can see it now.

RASHID: I did. He just stood there with that peculiar smile on his face, which I saw . . . do you know when?

SUNIL: Jammed, that's what it is. A touch of oil and it'll be loose again.

RASHID: Do you know when?

SUNIL: No, how would I know?

RASHID: When he left from here a few minutes back.

SUNIL: You're rushing to conclusions, aren't you?

RASHID: He is that kind of man.

SUNIL: Well my wife isn't that kind of woman. Now, let's try the engine shall we, and forget this silly talk.

RASHID: Yes, bwana.

fx: Car engine starts and runs

SUNIL: Ah, at last.

RASHID: Do you hear anything else?

SUNIL: I hear the rain and I hear some traffic on the main airport road, and perhaps an aeroplane high up.

RASHID: With such good ears you must hear what I hear too.

SUNIL: I can't hear what's in your imagination.

RASHID: Listen, there it is again!

Pause

SUNIL: You can't prove anything to me other than your own unhappiness. I am sorry for you.

RASHID: For me, not for yourself. (*Laughs*) There it is again, hidden in the wind: his laugh!

SUNIL: (*Shaken*) Shut up!

RASHID: Not so sure any longer. Ah, look, all the lights have gone off in your house. Must have got what he went there for. Food and drinks for us, wasn't it, bwana?

SUNIL: If I had a gun I'd shoot you!

RASHID: Why me, I haven't done anything.

SUNIL: Out of my way!

RASHID: It's too late, here he comes. (*Sound of Kamau whistling –*

approaching mic) Gay as a bird, that's what my wife used to say, gay as a bird. (*Whistling closer*) Admit it, bwana!

SUNIL: What?

RASHID: That your wife is no better than mine.

SUNIL: Never!

RASHID: While we have been here, something may have happened in there.

SUNIL: No!

RASHID: (*Getting at him*) But how will you ever know? (*Whistling louder*)

SUNIL: It's a lie, a dirty filthy lie. Shut up! (*Whistling stops abruptly*)

KAMAU: (*On mic*) Hello . . . something wrong? (*Silence*) I . . . I'm sorry I couldn't return earlier, but you saw the rain. It began raining again . . .

SUNIL: Get out, both of you – your car's ready.

KAMAU: What have you been up to, constable?

RASHID: Nothing. He just thinks he's better than us, superior in every way.

KAMAU: And yet his wife was so good to me.

RASHID: That worries him.

SUNIL: It doesn't worry me, but what did you do in there?

KAMAU: Nothing that she didn't want me to.

RASHID: Exactly!

KAMAU: The food and drinks are in the basket. Should we have some now?

SUNIL: Take it all and leave!

KAMAU: Constable, he's really angry. You're not telling me the truth.

RASHID: The truth, the sad truth, bwana Kamau, is that he no longer trusts his wife.

KAMAU: But I have great respect for her!

RASHID: He doubts if you respect any woman. Anyhow, let's go.

KAMAU: Wait a bit! Have you been telling him any more stories about me?

RASHID: That's all over. We are faced with this Asian threat now. Look at his cunning way of keeping silent while we argue among ourselves!

SUNIL: Your car is repaired. There isn't anything more I can do for you.

KAMAU: Come on, it's time we went.

RASHID: Anyway, he'll never know.

fx: Car doors open

KAMAU: Come on, constable!

fx: Car doors slam – car starts

(*Laughing and shouting*) We're good friends now, bwana mechanic. You and I. . . .

RASHID: (*Shouting*) You'll never know . . . you'll never know . . .

fx: Car pulls away fades into distance

Fade in

SUNIL: (*Shouting*) Devi, Devi . . . wake up!

DEVI: (*Sleepy*) Yes Sunil.

SUNIL: What did he do?

DEVI: Who, the inspector?

SUNIL: Yes, what did he do in here?

DEVI: He asked for food and drink, and I gave him what he wanted. Then we talked together for a while.

SUNIL: Yes, yes, I know all that.

DEVI: Then what do you mean?

SUNIL: Don't talk so much!

DEVI: What's come over you?

SUNIL: Nothing, what's come over you? Why don't you sit up and talk properly – instead of yawning! Suppose I told you that those were the thieves!

DEVI: No!

SUNIL: Why not?

DEVI: I . . . I don't know. I just can't think of Mr Kamau as a thief.

SUNIL: Ah ha!

DEVI: But you can easily find out.

SUNIL: How?

DEVI: By phoning the police.

SUNIL: No, I can't do that.

DEVI: Why not?

SUNIL: Because if they are members of the secret branch then the police won't tell us anything and if they were the thieves the police will suspect me for helping them. After all, we did let them go. (*Pause*) What should I do, Devi?

DEVI: Forget that it happened.

SUNIL: Is that the best way?

DEVI: I think so.

SUNIL: Then we'll never find out who they were or . . . anything else.

DEVI: (*Yawning*) They didn't rob us, Sunil. Why worry?

SUNIL: I do worry!

DEVI: (*Falling asleep*) What?

SUNIL: I said – what's the matter with you? (*Shakes her*) Wake up, Devi!

DEVI: (*Awake again – peeved*) What is it, Sunil – let me sleep!

SUNIL: Listen, answer me one question.

DEVI: One question . . . what is it?

SUNIL: Do you want to stay on, or do you want to leave this country – answer me that!

DEVI: It's up to you.

SUNIL: Then you want to stay on. (*Pause*) Please tell me the truth, Devi, the whole truth!

DEVI: That's the truth, Sunil . . . it's up to you . . . all up to you . . . (*Trails off into sleep*)

fx: Sound of heavy rain

SUNIL: She's asleep . . . My God, I'll never know anything . . . what am I to do?

fx: Peak howling wind and rain with hint of derisive laughter – fade out

The Soldiers

ROBIN WHITE

Robin White, *born in 1943 in Yorkshire, was educated there before taking a degree at Cambridge. He acted for a short time in repertory theatre in Britain before going to Cameroun for a year on V.S.O. as a teacher in 1966. On his return to Britain he joined the BBC African Service.* The Soldiers *was written especially for* African Theatre.

Recorded Sunday 28th June 1970

CAST
Daniel – Cosmo Pieterse
Mary – Tonie French
Mosquito 1 – Bloke Modisane
Mosquito 2 – Yemi Ajibade
Man – Alex Tetteh-Lartey

SOUND EFFECTS
Gunfire
Bottle
Broken glass
Chair
Dog's yelp
Car approaching
Car door slamming

Place: A country bar
Time: The present

fx: On mic – Sounds of clearing up. Bottles. Water etc.
    Off mic – Outside: Children playing and laughing. Shrieks

DANIEL: What now?
MARY: They've got a dog.
DANIEL: Teasing it?
MARY: Dropping it in an army of ants.
DANIEL: (*Sucks in breath through teeth*) Little brutes.

Pause

MARY: The children. They've changed too since the soldiers came.
    They were never so cruel before.
DANIEL: What are our two friends doing?
MARY: The soldiers?
DANIEL: Who else would I mean?
MARY: Sitting there. Watching. Laughing at the children. It was
    their idea.

fx: Dog yelps. Shriek of delight from children

DANIEL: How long have we got to put up with this?
MARY: They'll get tired of us soon.
DANIEL: It can't go on much longer. They're going to put us out
    of business.
MARY: How much do they owe?
DANIEL: More than three hundred beers they've had now.
MARY: (*Doubtful*) They might pay sometime.
DANIEL: With what? They haven't had a penny since the war
    finished.
MARY: (*Quietly*) Guns. You can get anything with guns.
DANIEL: What?
MARY: I said you can get anything with guns.
DANIEL: Oh, do something, woman. All afternoon you've been
    standing at that door. For God's sake do something. This
    place stinks.
MARY: What's the point? They'll be in again tonight. Fouling the
    place up.
DANIEL: Animals! Pigs!
MARY: Sh. They'll hear you.
DANIEL: Who cares? What else can they do to us?

MARY: They could shoot us.

DANIEL: (*Laughs*) Yes, they could always shoot us.

fx: More shrieks from children. Soldiers shouting

MARY: What if we closed down? Locked everything up till they went away?

DANIEL: What good would that do?

MARY: Well it might stop . . .

DANIEL: They'd break the doors down. Drink everything we've got. Turn the place into a latrine. I know them. Stupid grinning faces. Never wash. Never shave. War turns men into beasts, and then they turn *us* into beasts.

fx: Car in distance.

MARY: There's a car coming.

DANIEL: (*Still carried away*) Eh?

MARY: Someone's coming. A car. A new one.

DANIEL: More big men. I suppose they'll be stopping for free drinks too.

MARY: There's only one. He's alone.

DANIEL: And how many soldiers hiding in the boot?

fx: Car stops. Hooter

MARY: He's coming here.

DANIEL: Our lucky day.

MARY: Don't be rude to him, Daniel. He might be all right.

fx: Car door slam

DANIEL: No-one who drives a car is all right. They're all liars and cheats. Anyone with money in this country has got it by shitting on others.

MARY: Not everyone.

DANIEL: Everyone. There's not one who hasn't got his hand in someone else's pocket.

fx: Footsteps approaching mic

MARY: Sh. (*To man*) Welcome, Sir.

MAN: (*Coming in on mic*) La a get beer. (*Pause*) Bring de beer now. You no yere me?

DANIEL: We *can* speak English.

MAN: One beer. Cold. (*Pause*) Please.

fx: Bottle and glass slapped on to table – chair scrape as man sits

Educated, eh? There's nothing like education. Turns a man
into something.

DANIEL: Yes. Makes him fat.

MAN: (*Not hearing*) You should go into the city. Take up a career.
We need people like you. People with class. People with
manners. (*Pause. Sniffs*) What's the smell?

DANIEL: I smelled nothing till you came in.

MAN: Mind what you say, my friend.

DANIEL: (*Imitating*) Mind what you say. Mind what you say.
What kind of a country is this? 'Keep your mouth shut
country.' Don't say a thing, in case some big big man will
shit all over you.

MAN: Do you know who you're talking to?

DANIEL: I don't care who I'm talking to. One fat idiot is much
the same as the next.

MARY: Daniel. Please. Don't.

DANIEL: Shut up, woman.

MARY: What's he done to you?

DANIEL: What's he done to me? What hasn't he done? Him and
his kind. Bled this country white. Look at him – a bloated
elephant feeding off our labour.

MARY: (*To man*) I'm sorry. Please excuse him. He doesn't mean it.

DANIEL: You too, eh, woman? Bow to the big man. Open your
legs for him. He might fill you up with gold.

MARY: (*Cries*)

MAN: What's your name, my friend?

DANIEL: My name, eh? Going to report me? Going to send in
your little man to spy on me and lock me up? (*To wife*) Oh,
shut up, wife. What's the point of snivelling?

MARY: It was never like this before.

MAN: Before?

MARY: Before they came.

MAN: Who?

MARY: The soldiers.

MAN: Those two out there?

MARY: Yes.

MAN: What have they done?

DANIEL: (*Sarcastic*) Oh nothing. Nothing. They come here. Steal
our beer. Foul up the walls. Insult us. Corrupt the children.
It's nothing. Nothing at all. All part of the day's work.

MAN: Report them.

DANIEL: To who? To big men with fat bellies, who're only
    interested in keeping their jobs? Everyone's scared. No-one's
    going to stand up to the army.

MAN: (*Pompously*) There are democratic processes for dealing with
    this sort of thing.

DANIEL: Democratic processes all going by the name of bribery.

MAN: Democratic processes that I helped set up . . .

DANIEL: And are now benefiting from.

MAN: My friend, I am tired of people like you. People who mock
    our Government. (*As if making an official speech*) True . . .
    there are things wrong with our country . . . as with any
    other country . . . small things which will in due time be
    corrected. But the machinery is there . . . good machinery
    . . . there for the common people to use. Now take my
    advice, if these soldiers are misbehaving themselves, report
    them to the relevant government authorities.

DANIEL: All right. I report it to you. (*Like an army report*) Two
    soldiers are terrorizing our village. They're raping our women,
    and stealing our property. Could you please do something?
    Sar?

MAN: Unfortunately I can't.

DANIEL: What did I tell you? A big man like you. A man with
    a position. A man with a salary. And you can do nothing,
    like everyone else.

MAN: (*Uncomfortable*) Two weeks ago I could perhaps have done
    something . . .

DANIEL: But now?

MAN: (*Lying*) Er . . . I have resigned. I felt it was time to make
    way for newer . . . younger men.

DANIEL: (*Laughs*) I don't believe it. People like you don't resign.
    When they go, they're pushed.

fx: Outside off mic – shouts from soldiers: 'Out of the way, move, etc.'

MAN: What's that?

DANIEL: Our friends the soldiers.

MAN: What are they doing?

fx: Chair moves as man gets up

MARY: They're going to shoot the dog.

DANIEL: That'll put it out of its misery anyway.

MARY: Not with the gun they're going to use.

DANIEL: What gun is it?

MAN: A bren gun.

fx: Bren gun burst. Children run away shouting

Pause

Eh Yey. Yey. Look at the blood. It's everywhere.

fx: Soldiers laughing off mic

DANIEL: This whole village will be swimming in blood soon if no-one gets them out of here.

MARY: You'd better go.

MAN: Me? Why?

DANIEL: They're brutes – that's why.

MAN: I'm not frightened of them.

DANIEL: You haven't met them.

fx: From far off mic soldiers approach, singing 'All things bright and beautiful'

MARY: Go on. Drive off while you still have the chance.

DANIEL: One moment!

MAN: What?

DANIEL: Your beer. You haven't paid for your beer.

MARY: Let him go.

fx: Soldiers come in on mic still singing

DANIEL: Too late!

MOSQUITO 1: (*Abruptly stops singing*) Hey! Mosquito number two!

MOSQUITO 2: Yes, Mosquito number one?

MOSQUITO 1: Do you see what I see?

MOSQUITO 2: Where?

MOSQUITO 1: We have a visitor.

MOSQUITO 2: Isn't that nice. (*Laughs*)

MAN: I was just going.

MOSQUITO 1: Did you hear that, number two?

MOSQUITO 2: I heard him, number one.

MOSQUITO 1: I thought he said he was just going.

MOSQUITO 2: That's what I heard too.

MOSQUITO 1: Do you think he'll be leaving, number two?

MOSQUITO 2: (*Laughs*)

MAN: Get out of my way.

MOSQUITO 1: Sit down, fat man.

MAN: But . . .

MOSQUITO 1: Sit down.

fx: Sound of man pushed on to chair

   That's better. Now, may we join you?

MAN: Well, I . . .

MOSQUITO 1: Thank you, thank you. Eh, Mosquito number two.
   The man wants us to join him.

MOSQUITO 2: (*Laughs*)

fx: Bangs on table

MOSQUITO 1: Service. Beer. Beer. Bring beer.

MOSQUITO 2: Bring unto me all that travail and are heavy laden.
   And I will refresh you.

MOSQUITO 1: Beautifully put, number two. Beautifully put. (*To
   Daniel*) Didn't you think that was beautifully put, Mr
   Barman?

DANIEL: I'm not serving you.

MOSQUITO 1: Eh?

DANIEL: I'm not serving you.

MOSQUITO 1: Would you like to say that once more?

DANIEL: I said I'm not serving you.

MOSQUITO 1: He's like a gramophone record, number two. Keeps
   on saying the same thing over again.

MOSQUITO 2: Very boring.

DANIEL: I will not be bullied any more, by men with guns and
   no brains.

Pause

MOSQUITO 1: (*Laughs loudly, then abruptly stops*) I hate your kind,
   my friend. You and your small education. You and your
   morals. What's so marvellous about you? Eh? Have you ever
   seen a man with his head shot off, left in a ditch for the
   vultures? Did you volunteer to be blinded? All you did was
   sit here on your bottom in comfort, moaning about
   corruption in the city. Grumbling about all the taxes you've
   had to pay. Criticizing, criticizing, criticizing. Two weeks I've
   listened to your big mouth yap, yap, yapping. Now shut it!
   Do you think I risked my life so that you could sell beer to
   people like our fat friend here, who've filled their bellies
   while I was being shot at? No, my friend, you'll have to pay
   for this war like everyone else, and you can begin now by
   taking the tops off those bottles.

MOSQUITO 2: (*Applauds and cheers*) Speech! Speech! Mosquito number one for president! He speaks with cloven tongues, like as of fire.

MOSQUITO 1: Now bring that beer.

DANIEL: I will not.

MARY: Daniel, please, give it to him. Don't you see he's mad. He'll kill you.

Pause

MAN: (*Saving situation*) I'll buy the drinks. Drinks for everyone. Bring beer. I'll pay.

MOSQUITO 2: (*Laughing*) What a generous man! Faith, hope and charity, but the greatest of these is charity. May the good Lord smile on you, sir.

fx: Bottles opened – put on table

MOSQUITO 1: (*Calming down*) Do we know this kind man, Mosquito number two?

MOSQUITO 2: I think we do, number one.

MOSQUITO 1: Could it be Mr Mendwe?

MOSQUITO 2: Johnson Mendwe?

MOSQUITO 1: The politician?

MOSQUITO 2: The secretary of state?

MOSQUITO 1: The *ex* secretary of state.

Pause

MOSQUITO 2: Yes, number one. I think it's him.

MOSQUITO 1: I thought so.

Pause

MOSQUITO 2: Mosquito? Why did Mr Mendwe get the sack?

MOSQUITO 1: Well, there's a rumour, number two.

MOSQUITO 2: A rumour?

MOSQUITO 1: Only a rumour. We shouldn't repeat it.

MOSQUITO 2: No. It's bad to repeat rumours.

Pause

MOSQUITO 1: He stole Government property, number two.

MOSQUITO 2: Never!

MOSQUITO 1: Stole it and sold it back to the Government.

MOSQUITO 2: I don't believe it. People just don't do that kind of thing.

MOSQUITO 1: Guns, they say. He stole our guns while we were at the front being shot at. While we were waiting for those guns to defend ourselves.

MAN: It's a lie.

MOSQUITO 1: I beg your pardon? Did you speak?

MAN: I resigned. I retired. I didn't steal anything.

MOSQUITO 1: That's not what we heard. Not what we heard at all. Was it, number two?

MOSQUITO 2: No, number one, it wasn't.

MOSQUITO 1: Tell us the truth, Mr Mendwe.

MOSQUITO 2: The whole truth.

MOSQUITO 1: And nothing but the truth.

MOSQUITO 2: So help me God. (*Laughs*)

MAN: But I have told you the truth.

MOSQUITO 1: Have you?

MAN: Yes. Of course I have.

MOSQUITO 1: I don't think so.

MAN: (*Pause – thinking*) Like you, I got tired of politicians.

MOSQUITO 1: Oh yes.

MAN: I got sick of all the corruption. The bribery. The sickness of our system.

MOSQUITO 1: Really.

MAN: I decided to make way for the young. We need new blood in our Government . . .

MOSQUITO 1: Go on.

MAN: Young men like you. Young men with hope in them.

MOSQUITO 1: Hm.

MAN: Look, why am I bothering to talk to you like this? Who are you anyway?

MOSQUITO 1: We're nobody. Nobody at all.

MAN: There's no reason why I should have to justify myself to you.

MOSQUITO 1: No reason at all.

MAN: No.

MOSQUITO 1: Except that we've got the guns.

MAN: You won't use them. You wouldn't dare. Would you? You can't fool me.

MOSQUITO 1: Well, go on then. Walk out of the door. You'll soon find out if we intend to fire.

Pause

MOSQUITO 2: (*Chuckles*)

MAN: It's true. I got the sack.

MOSQUITO 1: That's better.

MAN: But I didn't steal the guns. I didn't steal the guns.

MOSQUITO 1: Then why did you get the sack?

MAN: I refused to play their game. I exposed them. I reported them. It wasn't me. It was them.

MOSQUITO 1: Who?

MAN: My bosses. Oh yes. I had bosses too. Breathing down my neck. Just like you.

MOSQUITO 1: And they used you as a scapegoat.

MAN: Yes.

MOSQUITO 1: They framed you.

MAN: Yes.

MOSQUITO 1: And sacrificed you to save their own skins.

MAN: Yes.

MOSQUITO 1: What do you think, number two? Do we believe him?

MOSQUITO 2: I don't know, number one.

MOSQUITO 1: It could be true, number two. These things do happen.

MOSQUITO 2: Yes, these things do happen. People can get framed.

MOSQUITO 1: But you don't believe him.

MOSQUITO 2: No.

MOSQUITO 1: Neither do I, number two.

MAN: You don't want to believe me.

MOSQUITO 1: Oh, I wouldn't say that.

MAN: You think that because I'm wearing a smart suit, and run a car, then I must be a cheat and a liar and a thief?

MOSQUITO 1: I've generally found that to be true, I must admit.

MAN: Almost everyone in Europe drives a car and wears a suit. Does that make them all liars and thieves?

MOSQUITO 1: I should think so. Yes.

MAN: Look. I'm just an ordinary man like you.

MOSQUITO 1: Hm!

MAN: I've a wife and family. All I want is peace.

MOSQUITO 1: Peace!

MAN: A simple life. That's all. With my family and friends.

MOSQUITO 1: We all want that, my friend. We all want that.

MAN: At home with the children. Away from the bitterness of the past.

MOSQUITO 1: It sounds beautiful.

MAN: Let's drink to the future. To the quiet life. The prosperous life. To the times of peace ahead.

MOSQUITO 1: Your wallet!

MAN: What?

MOSQUITO 1: Your wallet. Give me your wallet.

MAN: Why?

MOSQUITO 2: Do as you're told.

MAN There's nothing in it.

MOSQUITO 1: Nothing?

MAN: Just a few notes. Nothing much. Nothing worth having.

MOSQUITO 1: Give me it.

MAN: No. I can't.

MOSQUITO 1: I think you could. If you really tried you could.

MAN: Please. Don't take it. Please. I beg you.

MOSQUITO 1: He won't give us his wallet, number two.

MOSQUITO 2: Tut, tut, tut!

fx: Click of rifle bolt

MOSQUITO 1: Mr Mendwe. I think I ought to warn you. Mosquito here is very difficult to control. A nice boy, but he can get a little wild.

MOSQUITO 2: (*Laughs*) The wrath of the Lord will descend on you.

MAN: Here. Take it.

MOSQUITO 1: That's better. Thank you.

fx: Rustle of notes

MOSQUITO 1: Hey. Number two. Look at this. Hundreds.

MOSQUITO 2: Wonderful. So beautiful between the fingers. Soft and silky. Beautiful. (*Laughs softly to himself*)

MOSQUITO 1: (*Business-like*) Now, where did you get this?

MAN: It's mine.

MOSQUITO 1: Yours?

MAN: My salary.

MOSQUITO 1: Salary?

MAN: They owed me it.

MOSQUITO 1: Who?

MAN: The Government.

MOSQUITO 1: For what?

MAN: My work. My salary . . . in arrears. (*Pause*) They owed me it.

MOSQUITO 1: You stole it.

MAN: No.

MOSQUITO 1: Stuffed it in your pocket when you thought no-one was looking.

MAN: No.

MOSQUITO 1: Sneaked out of the door and ran off with it.

MAN: I didn't. It wasn't like that at all.

MOSQUITO 1: How was it then? Perhaps you got someone else to do your dirty work.

MAN: I promise you it's mine . . . my salary . . . they gave it me . . . please believe me.

MOSQUITO 1: Thief.

DANIEL: Leave him alone.

MOSQUITO 1: Shut up, you.

DANIEL: He's suffered enough.

MOSQUITO 1: I said shut up.

DANIEL: He's lost his job. Isn't that enough?

MOSQUITO 1: Did you hear me?

DANIEL: I heard you. Now leave him alone.

Pause

MOSQUITO 1: Mosquito number two!

MOSQUITO 2: (*Dreaming. Still fingering money*) Money. So beautiful. Like a woman. Soft and silky like a woman.

MOSQUITO 1: Hey! Mosquito! Wake up!

MOSQUITO 2: Sar!

MOSQUITO 1: Do you see what I see?

MOSQUITO 2: Where?

MOSQUITO 1: Through the window. Looking at us.

MOSQUITO 2: What?

MOSQUITO 1: A giraffe. A dangerous looking giraffe.

MOSQUITO 2: So there is.

MOSQUITO 1: Threatening to kill us, number two. Threatening to kill us.

MOSQUITO 2: (*Mock fear*) Help! Help! Help!

MOSQUITO 1: Action is called for, number two.

MOSQUITO 2: Now?

MOSQUITO 1: I'm afraid so.

MOSQUITO 2: (*Laughs*)

fx: Picks up gun. Click as it is cocked

MOSQUITO 2: Poor giraffe.

fx: Gun fire. Glass splintering

Pause

MOSQUITO 1: Mr Barman, you were saying?

DANIEL: I said, leave him alone. Can't you see he's had enough?

MARY: Daniel. Please. Don't go on.

DANIEL: They're pigs. They should be drowned in their own filth.

MOSQUITO 1: You'll apologize for that.

DANIEL: I'll apologize for nothing.

MOSQUITO 1: Number two!

MOSQUITO 2: Sar!

MOSQUITO 1: Behind the bar. On the shelf. Hiding behind the bottles. One elephant. Very dangerous.

MOSQUITO 2: Sar!

MOSQUITO 1: Range ten yards.

MOSQUITO 2: Sar!

MOSQUITO 1: Fire!

fx: Burst from bren gun. Bottles breaking, and smashing on the floor

MARY: Stop it! Stop it! Please. Stop it.

MOSQUITO 2: Elephant destroyed. Sar!

MOSQUITO 1: Well done, number two. (*To Daniel*) Now. Please carry on with what you were saying, Mr Barman. (*Pause*) Oh. He's lost his tongue, number two.

MOSQUITO 2: Struck dumb.

MOSQUITO 1: The mouth is shut.

MOSQUITO 2: A miracle. The good Lord has silenced him. Praise be to the Lord. (*Pause*) I'm thirsty.

MOSQUITO 1: (*Suddenly depressed. Speaking quite kindly*) Woman . . . Mrs . . . I forget your name . . . Mary . . . Bring more beer please. We're thirsty . . . all this shouting. And some water. Let me wash off this dog-blood.

fx: Bottles opened. Put on table

(*Slowly*) It's so boring here. Nothing to do all day but drink. Drink and talk to this fool of a soldier here. Brainless fool, who thinks only of women and food. I thought it would be all right after the war . . . After the fighting finished. They told us we'd be heroes . . . that's what they told us . . .

Heroes! Ha! Two hundred miles from home . . . no money
. . . no transport. Heroes! Look at us!

MAN: (*Trying to humour him*) Your home. Where is it?

MOSQUITO 1: My home is two feet under the ground, with worms
for company. (*Pause*) I had a friend . . .

MAN: (*Helping him*) A good friend?

MOSQUITO 1: A very good friend . . . he's dead.

MAN: Dead?

MOSQUITO 1: Yes, dead.

MAN: I am sorry.

MOSQUITO 1: We buried him . . . out there . . . what was left of
him. A hole in the ground for what was left of him.

MAN: Oh dear.

MOSQUITO 1: . . . It was hard. The ground . . . so hard. I
remember we couldn't dig deep enough . . . we . . .

MAN: I understand how you must feel.

MOSQUITO 1: (*Suddenly angry*) You understand nothing. Nothing
at all.

MAN: But I do.

MOSQUITO 1: All you understand is money. That's what you
want, isn't it? Your money back – that's what you want.
Pretending to be sympathetic because you want your money
back!

MOSQUITO 2: Beautiful money. Lovely and silky.

MAN: Look – keep the money. I give it to you. You deserve it.
You've served our country well.

MOSQUITO 1: My friend, you can't give us the money. We've
stolen it. Understand? We've stolen it. Just as we're going to
steal something else. Aren't we, number two?

MOSQUITO 2: (*Like a car hooter*) Poop. Poop.

MOSQUITO 1: Poop Poop.

MOSQUITO 2: Poop. Poop.

MAN: What do you mean – Poop Poop?

MOSQUITO 2: (*Car engine*) Voom. Voom.

MOSQUITO 1: Voom. Voom.

MOSQUITO 2: Poop Poop.

MOSQUITO 1: The car, where did you get the car?

MAN: It's mine. I bought it.

MOSQUITO 1: He says he bought it, number two.

MOSQUITO 2: Poop Poop.

MAN: But I did. Out of my own money I bought it.

MOSQUITO 2: Voom Voom.

MOSQUITO 1: I think it's Government property

MAN: It's not.

MOSQUITO 1: A ministry car.

MAN: No.

MOSQUITO 1: Paid for by the tax-payer.

MAN: No.

MOSQUITO 1: For official use only.

MAN: No.

MOSQUITO 1: With a chauffeur thrown in.

MAN: You're wrong. It's mine. I paid for it with my own money.
I promise you.

MOSQUITO 1: So you're denying it?

MAN: Of course I'm denying it.

MOSQUITO 1: Do you hear that, Mosquito? He's denying it.

MOSQUITO 2: Poop Poop. Poop Poop. Voooooom.

MOSQUITO 1: I'm afraid we don't believe you.

MAN: But you must. I'm speaking the truth.

MOSQUITO 1: Number two here's convinced you stole it. Aren't
you, number two?

MOSQUITO 2: Poop.

MOSQUITO 1: You see. He's certain of it.

MAN: Look. You must believe me. I'll show you the receipts.

MOSQUITO 1: Receipts?

MAN: For the car. Receipts from the garage where I bought
it.

MOSQUITO 1: Forged.

MAN: Take a look at them. I've got them here.

MOSQUITO 1: Forged.

MAN: You can't forge receipts.

MOSQUITO 1: Can't you?

MAN: Of course you can't.

MOSQUITO 1: I think *you* could. I think you could do anything
where money is concerned.

MAN: *(Shouting)* I didn't forge them. Once and for all, I didn't
forge them.

MOSQUITO 1: Don't shout.

MAN: I'm not shouting.

MOSQUITO 1: You're not whispering.

MAN: I'll shout if I want to shout.

MOSQUITO 1: All right. Have a good shout. Go on. We don't

mind at all. Clear your lungs out. Get rid of all that
frustration. Go on. Shout as much as you like.

Pause

MAN: What do you want from me?
MOSQUITO 1: I don't know. What do we want from him, number
two?
MOSQUITO 2: Voooom.
MOSQUITO 1: The car. I think he wants the car. Is that right,
Mosquito? You want the car?
MOSQUITO 2: Poop.
MAN: All my money. You've taken all my money . . . And now
you want the car.
MOSQUITO 1: I'm afraid so.
MAN: I can't. How will I get home?
MOSQUITO 1: How are *we* going to get home?
MAN: They're expecting me.
MOSQUITO 1: Oh yes.
MAN: My people. They're expecting me. They've prepared a
reception for me.
MOSQUITO 1: What a shame.
MAN: There'll be food and drink. For weeks they've been looking
forward to it. I can't let them down. Please.
DANIEL: Let him go.
MARY: You don't want the car. Not really.
MOSQUITO 1: Don't we?
DANIEL: Of course you don't.
MOSQUITO 1: Mosquito wants it.
MARY: But he has to be home. His people will worry.
MOSQUITO 1: Mosquito's always wanted a car. All his life he's
wanted a car. Haven't you, Mosquito?
MOSQUITO 2: Poop.
MOSQUITO 1: Ever since he was a child. That's been his ambition
To sit behind a wheel and blow the hooter.
MOSQUITO 2: Poop.
MARY: Let him go. You only wanted to frighten him, that's all.
You don't want the car. Not really. Let him go now

Pause

MOSQUITO 1: It's getting dark. The children have gone home.
MARY: You've frightened them with your shooting.

MOSQUITO 1: Hm!

MARY: You have. You've frightened the whole village. Before you came this bar was full of people every night. Ten, twenty, sometimes fifty people drinking and laughing.

MOSQUITO 1: We're bad for business, eh?

MARY: It's not that.

MOSQUITO 1: What then? What else is there besides making money?

MARY: Our children were innocent before you came.

MOSQUITO 1: Hah!

MARY: Well, it's true. They were.

MOSQUITO 1: I've seen a child. A child no more than eight years old, pick up a rifle and shoot a soldier in the face. Don't talk to me about innocence.

MARY: That was war. That's what war does to people.

MOSQUITO 1: War shows you what people are really like.

MARY: But we can't go on like that. It's over. Finished.

MOSQUITO 1: And what about me? What do you expect me to do? Forget about it? Forget that I saw all these things? Pretend that it never happened?

Pause. Mosquito 2 sings softly to himself

MARY: You must try.

MOSQUITO 1: I can't.

MARY: Why not?

MOSQUITO 1: There's nothing else I can do. I'm not trained for anything. All I know is how to kill people.

MARY: Begin again. Learn something else.

MOSQUITO 1: There's no going back. It's here in my head. I can't forget it.

MARY: You must. Life goes on.

Pause

MOSQUITO 1: Nothing will be any good again.

MARY: It will.

MOSQUITO 1: Not till *we're* gone. Not till we're out of the way. We're no use any more. The country needs builders, not fighters.

MARY: Your pride's hurt, that's all.

MOSQUITO 1: What do I care about my pride?

MARY: You're upset because people aren't impressed with you

any more. Now that the war's over, you're no-one, and you
don't like it.

MOSQUITO 1 : Don't talk nonsense.

MARY : It's true. Two months ago everyone looked up to you. A
man in uniform! The pride of the country! Now you're just
a man and you don't like it.

MOSQUITO 1 : Get away from me, woman. What do you know
about anything?

MARY : Put your guns away. You don't need them any more.
You said yourself we want builders now.

MOSQUITO 1 : I'm not a builder. I'm a soldier.

MARY : There's nothing wonderful about being a soldier. Anyone
can be a soldier. There's no skill in pulling a trigger to kill.

MOSQUITO 1 : Isn't there?

MARY : Of course there isn't.

MOSQUITO 1 : You don't know. You weren't there. You never
had to kill anyone.

Pause

MARY : Your friend's asleep. Look at him. He's only a baby
really.

MOSQUITO 1 : Yes. He never grew up. Never will.

MARY : Take him away from here. Take him home.

MOSQUITO 1 : I can't tell him what to do.

MARY : Yes, you can. He follows you around like a dog.

MOSQUITO 1 : But the dog can bite.

Pause

You're not saying much, Mr Barman.

DANIEL : No.

MOSQUITO 1 : That's not like you.

DANIEL : I don't talk unless I've something interesting to say.

MOSQUITO 1 : Meaning that what we've been saying isn't
interesting?

DANIEL : I've no time for sentimental nonsense.

MOSQUITO 1 : Me? Sentimental?

DANIEL : Yes. You sounded like a couple of lovebirds cooing
away together.

MOSQUITO 1 : What's the matter with you?

DANIEL : Nothing's the matter with me.

MOSQUITO 1 : Then relax.

DANIEL: I'll relax when I see your backside disappearing down that road.

MOSQUITO 1: (*Laughs*) I don't understand you. Why are you so rude to everyone?

MARY: It's because of the war. All the killing that's been going on. All the corruption. It's made him bitter.

MOSQUITO 1: I don't think so. I think he's jealous. Jealous of people like our fat friend here. You'd like to be a big man too, wouldn't you? You'd like to have a motor car. Like to have a big salary. Like to have power. You're just like everyone else really, aren't you?

DANIEL: If you say so. I'm not arguing with you.

MOSQUITO 1: (*Laughs*) All right. Keep up the big moral act if it makes you feel better.

DANIEL: I will.

Pause

MOSQUITO 1: (*To man*) What are *you* doing here?

MAN: Me?

MOSQUITO 1: Yes, you. What are you doing here?

MAN: You told me to . . .

MOSQUITO 1: Get out.

MAN: What?

MOSQUITO 1: I said go. Leave. Get out of here. I can't stand the sight of you. You're fouling up the air.

fx: Chair scrape as man gets up

MAN: Yes . . . thank you . . . that's very kind . . .

MOSQUITO 1: (*Shouting*) Get out!

MAN: Thank you very much.

MOSQUITO 1: Stop cringing.

MAN: Let's all shake hands. All of us.

MOSQUITO 1: Take your smelly sweaty hands off me.

MOSQUITO 2: (*Waking up*) Poop Poop.

MAN: (*Going off mic*) Well . . . goodbye.

MARY: Goodbye.

MOSQUITO 2: Hey! Stop! Where's he going? My car!

MOSQUITO 1: It's all right, Mosquito. Let him go. We've got his money.

MARY: Go on. While you have the chance. Run.

MOSQUITO 2: My car! He's stealing my car! Get off me!
MOSQUITO 1: Mosquito! It's me. Your friend. Trust me.

fx: Chair scrape as Mosquito 2 gets up

MOSQUITO 2: You promised me. You promised me the car.

fx: Scuffle. Gun cocked

MOSQUITO 1: Mosquito! Stop!

fx: Gunfire. Man screams off mic

Pause

MARY: He's dead.
MOSQUITO 1: Mosquito . . . why?
MOSQUITO 2: My car. You promised me.
MOSQUITO 1: Oh, Mosquito.
DANIEL: You pig! You stupid pig! You animal. You stupid
    pig-headed animal!
MOSQUITO 2: Shut up!
DANIEL: (*Hysterical*) You're all the same, you soldiers! Filth! All
    of you! Filth!
MOSQUITO 2: Shut up! Shut up!
MOSQUITO 1: Easy, Mosquito. Calm down.
DANIEL: You're pigs!
MOSQUITO 2: (*Trying to control himself*) Tell him to stop it,
    number one. Tell him to stop shouting at me.
DANIEL: Pigs! Pigs! Pigs! Pigs!
MOSQUITO 1: Mosquito, don't. Put it down. Do you hear me?
    Put it down. Number two, I beg you, don't! Please!

fx: Gunfire. Many shots. Screams. Glass breaking

Pause – dead silence

fx: More shots

Pause – dead silence

MOSQUITO 1: Mosquito. Why? Why did you do it? Why?
MOSQUITO 2: Poop. Poop.
MOSQUITO 1: Mosquito. You killed them. Three people dead.
MOSQUITO 2: Poop.

fx: Face slap from Mosquito 1 to Mosquito 2

MOSQUITO 1: Stop it, Mosquito! Stop it! Answer me!

MOSQUITO 2: He shouted at me, number one. He shouldn't have shouted at me.

MOSQUITO 1: Oh, Mosquito.

MOSQUITO 2: I'm sorry, number one. I'm sorry.

Pause

fx: Sounds of broken bottles being kicked

MOSQUITO 2: The car. Is it mine? (*Pause*) You promised me the car. You said I could have it. (*Pause*) Number one. Talk to me, number one. (*Pause*) The car. May I take it, number one?

MOSQUITO 1: Take it.

MOSQUITO 2: Are you sure, number one?

MOSQUITO 1: Take it. It's yours, Mosquito.

Pause

MOSQUITO 2: Well . . . I'll go then. (*Pause*) (*Going off mic*) Goodbye . . . number one . . . goodbye.

fx: Footsteps going off mic. Car door slams

MOSQUITO 1: (*Cries*)

Slow fade out

The Trial of Busumbala

GABRIEL J. ROBERTS

Gabriel J. Roberts, *born in Bathurst in 1926, was educated in the Gambia before doing a teacher training course in Ghana and then gaining a degree in English and Philosophy from St Andrew's University, Scotland. He is now Chief Education Officer in the Gambia, and writes often for the* West African Journal of Education. *He has had a number of his plays produced in the Gambia, but* The Trial of Busumbala *is the first to have been broadcast and published.*

Recorded Sunday 2nd August 1970

CAST

Judge – Alex Tetteh-Lartey
Prosecuting Counsel – Louis Mahoney
Defence Counsel – Cosmo Pieterse
Maxwell Armitage – Lionel Ngakane
Mohammadu Casterbridgia – Femi Euba
Sambang Sambou – John Sorbah-Green
Sergeant ⎫
Sales Manager ⎬ – Peter Otai
Spectators and other parts played by members of the cast

Place: The Supreme Court, Bathurst, the Gambia. The Court is assembled
Time: 1962

fx: Fade in court atmosphere *with speech*

PROSECUTION: My lord, Members of the Jury, on the very last
    night in the month of January, in the year of Our Lord
    nineteen hundred and sixty-two between the hours of
    eleven-thirty and midnight, Mr Maxwell Armitage, the
    Principal of Armitage School, reported at the Police Station,
    in Georgetown, MacCarthy Island Division, that his brand
    new Telefunken radio set had disappeared from his house.
    Thirty minutes later, a man with a Telefunken radio set was
    seen crossing the Bakang Jato Bridge from Georgetown and
    going in the direction of Sankoli Kunda. This man was later
    identified as Marafan Busumbala, the accused, and the radio
    set subsequently verified by Messrs Tangalsahol Ltd, the
    Bathurst Agents, as the radio set sold to the said Principal of
    Armitage School on the 13th September 1961. Before going
    any further, my lord, I would like to establish more ostensibly
    the facts I have just rehearsed to the Court, by examining
    two witnesses. The first witness is the Sales Manager, Messrs
    Tangalsahol Ltd.

SERGEANT: (*Calling*) Sales Manager, Messrs Tangalsahol Ltd!

SALES MANAGER: (*Coming on mic*) Yes. Yes, I'm coming. Now
    then, yes, 'I swear by Almighty God that what I am about
    to say is the sacred truth and no cock-and-bull story. So help
    me God'.

PROS: What is your name?

SALES MANAGER: Banjul Tangalsahol.

PROS: What is your occupation?

SALES MANAGER: Business.

PROS: Can you be more specific than that?

SALES MANAGER: Sales Manager, Messrs Tangalsahol, Ltd.

PROS: Thank you. Did you on the 13th September 1961, sell a
    Telefunken radio set to Mr Maxwell Armitage, the principal
    of Armitage School?

SALES MANAGER: I posted one such set to him on the Fulladu
    that left Bathurst on that date.

PROS: I am much obliged to you. Learned counsel for the defence,
    the witness is yours.

DEFENCE: What is the registered number of the Telefunken radio set you sold to Mr Maxwell Armitage?

SALES MANAGER: (*Reeling it off*) PRW/ETJ1984/WX61.

DEFENCE: You must, sir, have a phenomenal memory to have such a complicated number so clearly registered in your mind. Do you keep in your head the numbers of all the sets you sell to customers?

PROS: My lord, I'm sure that is an unfair question.

DEFENCE: It is no matter. Did Mr Maxwell Armitage acknowledge the receipt of the set?

SALES MANAGER: No.

DEFENCE: That is all, my lord.

JUDGE: The witness may step down.

fx: Footsteps going off mic

PROS: I would like, my lord, to examine the principal witness, Mr Maxwell Armitage himself.

SERGEANT: (*Calling*) Maxwell Armitage!

fx: Measured footsteps coming on mic

ARMITAGE: Yes, please. Ah yes – thank you my man but I know the proper oath – I have no need of a card! 'I swear by Almighty God that the evidence I give shall be the truth, the whole truth, and nothing but the truth – so help me God.' You see! Now then, what do you want to know?

PROS: What is your name?

ARMITAGE: What do you want to know for?

PROS: To inform the Court.

ARMITAGE: Haven't you done so already?

PROS: No. That's why I've called you.

ARMITAGE: How did you call me?

PROS. Maxwell Armitage.

ARMITAGE: Ah well, that's just part of my name.

PROS: Your complete name?

ARMITAGE: I am Maxwell Armitage Esq., M.A., Ph.D., C.M.G., the most intellectual of intellectuals; the supreme . . .

PROS: That will do . . . that will do. Is this all part of your name?

ARMITAGE: These are the words by which I am known.

PROS: What is your job?

ARMITAGE: My job? You mean my profession, surely.

PROS: Yes, your profession.

ARMITAGE: I belong to the most noble order of the teaching
    profession.

PROS: I see. Is that what you do at Armitage? You belong . . .

ARMITAGE: . . . to the most noble order of the teaching profession.

PROS: What post do you hold at Armitage?

ARMITAGE: As the most intellectual of intellectuals, I am the
    supreme leader of the staff of Armitage School.

PROS: Are you the Headmaster?

ARMITAGE: You may call me the Principal.

PROS: Thank you. So you are the Principal of Armitage School.

ARMITAGE: That is a valid deduction.

PROS: (*Impatiently*) Are you?

ARMITAGE: Yes.

PROS: Thank you. What did you do on the night of the 31st
    January 1962.

ARMITAGE: I slept like a log.

PROS: You are behaving like a log.

ARMITAGE: I beg your pardon?

PROS: Did you call at the police station in Georgetown?

ARMITAGE: I did.

PROS: Why?

ARMITAGE: I went to acquaint the Superintendent of the mysterious
    disappearance of my brand-new Telefunken radio set.

PROS: Are you able to identify your own particular set from
    among others of the same model?

ARMITAGE: Certainly!

PROS: There are three sets on the table over there. Will you
    please select your own set from among them?

ARMITAGE: This is the one.

PROS: That is all, my lord.

DEFENCE: What is the registered number of your radio set?

ARMITAGE: (*Not expecting this question*) Let me see . . . (*Gives the
    impression he is thinking very hard*) PRW/ETJ1984/WX62.
    That's it.

PROS: Are you sure that is the correct number?

ARMITAGE: Oh yes. Positive.

PROS: Thank you, Mr Armitage. I have no further questions.

DEFENCE: And I have no questions to put to Mr Armitage *yet*,
    my lord. Except to confirm the number of your set, Mr
    Armitage: you did say PRW/ETJ1984/WX62?

ARMITAGE: (*Exploding*) I did, I've said it twice. Really, I must
   protest, my lord, at this . . .
DEFENCE: Thank you, Mr Armitage, that will be all for now.

fx: Measured footsteps going off mic

JUDGE: Very well then, we will proceed with the case.
   Gentlemen of the Jury, I am satisfied that there is a case
   before us. As we proceed, therefore, in our investigation, I
   would like you to bear in mind that it is the character of a
   citizen which is at stake. It is in his best interest and in the
   interest of Justice that every evidence in his favour should be
   given the consideration it deserves. But while it is incumbent
   on you to protect him against any unjust charge brought
   against him, you are legally and morally bound to weigh and
   consider every aspect of the case before taking the plunge of
   decision. The Counsel for the Defence is now at liberty to
   present his case.
DEFENCE: My lord, members of the Jury, I do not intend to
   attempt to disprove the plaintiff has indeed lost a radio set
   and that a radio set was in fact removed from his house on
   the night in question by the accused, my client. What I
   would like to make abundantly clear is the fine courage of
   the accused and the nobility of his action (*Murmurs of
   surprise*) that has been so much the object of disparagement
   by the Prosecution.
   The accused, a Member of the House of Representatives and
   a champion of the bourgeois population of Georgetown, had
   invariably in the past three months received complaints from
   the members of his constituency that the said plaintiff had the
   intolerable habit of tuning his radio so diabolically loud that
   it was impossible to hear oneself when conversing in any of
   the neighbouring houses without inflicting undue strain upon
   the ear drum or the vocal chords. It was, therefore, in the
   interest of humanity in general and the immediate
   neighbours of the said plaintiff in particular that the said
   accused was reluctantly driven to remove the devilish set
   from the house in question.
   I would like, my lord, to draw your attention and the
   attention of the Jury to Clause 13 of Criminological Treaties
   Volume III, written by the great authority on criminal
   investigations, Sir Gustavus Lotramello, Q.C., and published

by the Banjul Press. In this magnum opus Sir Gustavus writes: 'When an act which in ordinary circumstances may be considered criminal is shown beyond all reasonable doubt to be the outcome of pure necessity and motivated solely by altruistic or humanitarian considerations, such an act may, at the discretion of the Court, be divested of all criminal connotations and redound to the credit of the agent or agents associated with the commission of the said act.'

I would like, my lord, at this stage to examine two witnesses together with the principal witness for the Prosecution. I would examine Momodou Casterbridgia, first.

SERGEANT: *(Calling)* Momodou Casterbridgia!

fx: Footsteps approaching mic

C'BRIDGIA: Man dali.

JUDGE: Would the witness require an interpreter?

C'BRIDGIA: I am thanking your Excellency for your good will and generosity reply offer but I can incomprehend the English language like anyone in Georgetown or Bathurst besides. I was educated at the Methodist School in MacCarthy.

SERGEANT: Your Honour, the witness does not require an interpreter.

C'BRIDGIA: No, no.

SERGEANT: Would you hold this Bible please?

C'BRIDGIA: I am not a Christian man.

SERGEANT: The Koran?

C'BRIDGIA: I no swear by the Koran, I swear to my honour. *(In a prayerful mood)* I swear by mine honour most respectfully to transmit the intelligency knowledge respectively concern the stealing of the radio set.

fx: There is a current of undertones, then the Sergeant clicks his heels smartly

SERGEANT: Silence in Court!!

There is perfect silence

JUDGE: Counsel may proceed.

DEFENCE: What is your name?

C'BRIDGIA: My name is entitled Mohammadu Casterbridgia.

DEFENCE: Where do you live?

C'BRIDGIA: Opposed to the Police Station in Georgetown, MacCarthy Island Division.

DEFENCE: What is your job?

C'BRIDGIA: I have been in the public beneficial for good thirteen years back.

JUDGE: What is that?

DEFENCE: The witness means, my lord, he has been serving the Georgetown Community for thirteen years.

JUDGE: That is not what he says.

C'BRIDGIA: I means what I says.

JUDGE: You must say what you mean.

DEFENCE: Were you ever disturbed by the sound of a radio set owned by the Principal of Armitage School?

C'BRIDGIA: Every day.

DEFENCE: What did you do about it?

C'BRIDGIA: I forwarded my petition directly through my candidate and imperatively commanded that the set be removed for the public beneficiary.

DEFENCE: Whom do you speak of as 'my candidate'?

C'BRIDGIA: The Hon. Marafan Busumbala.

DEFENCE: That is all, my lord.

PROS: Do you understand English?

C'BRIDGIA: (*Annoyed*) Of course I do!

PROS: Well that, sir, is the first correct English you have spoken this morning. (*Pause*) I wish to put it to you that you are the most idiotic person I have met. (*The witness is muttering in Mandinka*) The depth of ignorance into which you have fallen is almost beyond the limit of human comprehension. (*Witness is getting more furious and the court audience is getting excited*) Your plight is made even worse by your inability to comprehend your own ignorance.

The Prosecution is obviously making all this up to irritate the witness; the latter is by this time beside himself and rattling sonorous Mandinka and the Court spectators are getting out of hand

SERGEANT: Silence in Court!

Dead silence

DEFENCE: I would appeal to you, my lord, for the protection of the witness.

JUDGE: I suggest that the Prosecution Counsel proceed in more direct terms to his cross-examination of the witness.

PROS: I wish to establish, my lord, that the witness is incapable of giving reliable answers to questions put to him in English. I suggest that an interpreter be employed.

JUDGE: The witness has already been offered an interpreter. Do you wish to proceed with your cross-examination or not?

PROS: (*Resigns himself to the situation*) Very well, my lord. To what political party do you belong?

C'BRIDGIA: Enlightened People's Congress.

PROS: I see. Do you attend functions at Armitage School? Are you usually invited to their plays and concerts?

C'BRIDGIA: No.

PROS: Thank you. That is all my lord.

JUDGE: The witness may step down.

fx: Footsteps going off mic

DEFENCE: My lord, I would like to call now Sambang Sambou.

SERGEANT: (*Calling*) Sambang Sambou!

fx: Sambou's footsteps coming on mic

SAMBOU: Yes please.

SERGEANT: Here is the oath card, Mr Sambou.

SAMBOU: (*Rattling it off*) I swear by Almighty God that the evidence I give shall be the truth, the whole truth, and nothing but the truth. Yes Sir.

DEFENCE: What is your name?

SAMBOU: Sambang Sambou.

DEFENCE: Where do you live?

SAMBOU: Jackson Street. At the Armitage Staff Compound.

DEFENCE: What is your occupation?

SAMBOU: Teaching. I am on the staff of Armitage School.

DEFENCE: Have you ever been disturbed by the sound of a radio belonging to the Principal of your school?

SAMBOU: I am very sorry to say this about my immediate Head, but I have had several dissertations with him on the subject of the conflict between individual and social rights and still he always gives the impression that he cares little about the rest of the world around him. If everyone disregarded the existence of everyone else, surely society would be impossible.

JUDGE: Will the witness please give more direct answers to questions from the Counsel.

SAMBOU: My lord, I didn't want it to appear I am betraying my trust as a member of the staff of Armitage School or that I have a grudge or any personal grievance against my boss. On the contrary, I am very happy at Armitage, though I must confess I was much happier when the radio set was stolen. I find it extremely difficult to do any constructive thinking in a noisy atmosphere.

JUDGE: Mr Sambou (*Pause*) I believe you mentioned not so long ago that you are a teacher at Armitage School. Armitage teachers are well known for their respect for the logic of words and their precision in speech. Will you please be precise on this occasion and tell the Court whether or not you have been disturbed by the radio in question?

SAMBOU: I have, your Honour, been trying to say this all the time.

JUDGE: (*Somewhat sternly*) Have you or have you not?

SAMBOU: I have, your Honour.

JUDGE: Thank you.

DEFENCE: Thank *you*, my lord. (*To the witness*) How often have you been so disturbed?

SAMBOU: Several times. Almost every night while he had the set.

DEFENCE: Where were you on the night of 31st January 1962?

SAMBOU: I had supper at 8 p.m. and was at my house up to 11.5 when I left for the Staff Library in search of a quiet spot to read and meditate.

DEFENCE: Why did you have to go to the Library to do this?

SAMBOU: Because I couldn't read or meditate in my own house, which is right opposite the Principal's, and the noise from his radio was on that particular night far too disturbing to concentrate in.

DEFENCE: Did you ever hear others complain about this set?

SAMBOU: All the Armitage Staff. We have discussed him in the Staff Room several times and have presented him on one occasion with a Declaration of Rights, with the hope he might show more concern for the happiness of others and be less disturbing in the use of his set. But alas! All our efforts were in vain. Moreover, the Old Man always insisted we must be efficient in everything we did, whether it was the

preparation of our lesson notes, the delivery of our lessons or
the supervision of extra-curricular activities, but . . .

JUDGE: Will you please go straight to the point, Mr Sambou.

DEFENCE: My lord, (*Pause*) I would like to hear more from the
witness. (*Pause*) As you were saying. (*Turning in the direction of
the witness and giving him a signal to continue*)

SAMBOU: (*Responding to the signal*) As I was saying, the Old Man
is always very fussy about proficiency in everything, but he
would never give us the ghost of a chance to prepare our
lessons or feed our minds in anything like a congenial
atmosphere.

DEFENCE: (*Observing that the Judge is not taking down the statement
of the witness*) My lord, I would request a repetition of the
last sentence of the witness.

JUDGE: I didn't think it was relevant.

DEFENCE: I have great respect for your judgment, my lord, but
what you have omitted may prove to be a missing link in
your final address to the Jury. I would suggest that the
sentence be repeated by the witness and, in this connection,
I would direct your attention, my lord, to Section 36 of the
Supreme Court Procedure, Volume LIII, lines 3 and 4.

JUDGE: (*Realizes that the Counsel is right and is somewhat apologetic*) If
the Counsel feels the recording of the statements are not an
undue waste of time, I would ask the witness to repeat his
last sentence and proceed with his story.

DEFENCE: Thank you, my lord.

SAMBOU: (*Responding to a signal from the Counsel*) The Old Man
would not give us a chance to prepare our lessons in a
congenial atmosphere. Sometimes I would make bold to
challenge him like a man, but he is the most dogmatic
person I have ever worked with. He would simply brush me
aside with 'Rubbish! There is no such thing as peace and
quietness; the world is full of noises, great ones and little
ones'. Just like that! He is so unfathomable!

DEFENCE: Going back to the night of the 31st January, do you
remember what programme the Principal had on at about
11 p.m., when you left your house for the Staff Library?

SAMBOU: Trumpet music. It sounded like Louis Armstrong, but
I discovered a few minutes later that it wasn't. In fact, the
Old Man was very cross that I mistook Handel for
Armstrong.

DEFENCE: You said 'a few minutes later'? (*Pause*) Am I to understand that a few minutes after leaving your house you were met by Mr Maxwell Armitage who pointed out to you that you were listening to a Trumpet voluntary from Handel and not a jazz piece from Louis Armstrong?

SAMBOU: That is correct.

DEFENCE: Where did you encounter Mr Armitage?

SAMBOU: In the Library.

DEFENCE: The Staff Library?

SAMBOU: Yes.

DEFENCE: It follows then that Mr Armitage could not have been at his house at 11.10.

SAMBOU: That is so. He was in the Library and did not leave it until about 11.30 when he remarked casually that the BBC programme was probably over.

DEFENCE: And all this time, that is before 11.30 p.m., the radio was on?

SAMBOU: At full blast. When he left the library, however, the music had stopped.

DEFENCE: That is all, my lord.

Pause

PROS: Now, Mr Sambou. To what political party do you belong?

SAMBOU: None, in particular.

PROS: Do you sympathize with the political standpoint of any particular party?

SAMBOU: Yes, I do.

PROS: Which one is it?

SAMBOU: The Enlightened People's Congress.

PROS: Thank you. How long have you been teaching?

SAMBOU: Twelve years.

PROS: Is this a continuous or broken service?

SAMBOU: It was broken for three months two years ago.

PROS: What did you do during this period of three months?

SAMBOU: I was standing as a candidate at the last General Election.

PROS: For what constituency?

SAMBOU: Georgetown, MacCarthy Island Division.

PROS: What party?

SAMBOU: (*As though the question is absurd*) Enlightened People's

Congress, of course! I cannot tolerate the idealism of the Progress Party.

PROS: Thank you. Do you have other interests apart from teaching and politics?

SAMBOU: Acting and producing plays.

PROS: That requires a good deal of creative imagination. In fact the ability to think imaginatively is an essential qualification for any actor, amateur or professional.

SAMBOU: I quite agree with you.

PROS: Being an actor, then, you are able to imagine things that have not really taken place. You can see a horse run across a battlefield in France. You can hear the sound of trumpets, the calls of the bugle, the shouts of a mob, and yet these may not actually be taking place.

SAMBOU: The actor's mind can certainly be trained to such perfection.

PROS: Don't you sometimes dream about things as though you were on the stage acting them?

SAMBOU: Sometimes I do, especially when the date of the performance is very near.

PROS: Haven't you sometimes thought about these things in your waking moments as well? (*Pause*) When you teach history for example, or drama, don't you sometimes find yourself involuntarily behaving as though you were actually on the stage or on the battlefield of France, talking to the French king's messenger? Don't you, Mr Sambou, on occasions suddenly react as though you were hearing the blasts of a trumpet or the shoutings of a mob?

SAMBOU: (*Rather uncertainly*) Occasionally, yes.

PROS: Is it not possible then that you might on the night of 31st January have been carried away by one of these flights of imagination when you thought you heard Louis Armstrong on the trumpet, or the trumpets in the *Messiah*, as you later intimated? Is it not possible, sir, that what you heard or imagined you heard did not in fact come from the Telefunken radio set of Mr Maxwell Armitage?

SAMBOU: (*Too late to detect the trap into which he has been led*) Certainly not!

PROS: That is all, my lord.

DEFENCE: My lord.

JUDGE: Counsel for the defence may proceed.

DEFENCE: Mr Sambou, when you said 'certainly not', did you mean that it was not possible for you to have imagined the sound from Mr Armitage's radio set, or that what you heard did not in fact come from the set?

SAMBOU: I did not imagine anything! I heard the trumpet with my very ears as though it was right under my roof.

DEFENCE: Thank you. You may step down, Mr Sambou!

fx: Footsteps going off mic

I would like, my lord, to examine again the Principal Prosecution witness, Mr Maxwell Armitage.

SERGEANT: (*Calling*) Mr Maxwell Armitage!

fx: Armitage's footsteps coming on mic

ARMITAGE: Yes please. Ah . . . (*slowly and with feeling*) . . . I swear by Almighty God that the evidence . . .

JUDGE: There's no need to repeat your oath, Mr Armitage!

ARMITAGE: (*Crestfallen and disappointed at not being able to show off again*) Oh! Well, my lord, I thought that . . .

JUDGE: No need to think, Mr Armitage, we heard you the first time. (*Laughter*) Counsel for the defence may proceed.

DEFENCE: Thank you, my lord. You are the Principal of Armitage School?

ARMITAGE: Not again!

DEFENCE: Are you?

ARMITAGE: Yes.

DEFENCE: Have you ever been approached by any or some members of your staff on matters pertaining to the use of your radio set?

ARMITAGE: I have endeavoured to explain to these young friends of mine the delights one could derive from listening to good music. And when an orchestral piece is on it's no use having your radio low; you won't hear some of the instruments if you do. Moreover, to get the impression you are in a great concert hall, you must tune it at maximum volume. I . . .

DEFENCE: Answer my question, please. Have you ever been approached about the use of your radio set?

ARMITAGE: Yes, I have.

DEFENCE: You have had complaints about the inconvenience your cherished radio set had been causing other people. What did you do about it?

ARMITAGE: Well, that was what I was trying to explain to you, but . . .

DEFENCE: (*Losing his temper*) Did you do anything about reducing the volume of your radio?

ARMITAGE: Why should I?

DEFENCE: (*Exploding*) Don't ask questions! Answer them!

ARMITAGE: (*Very calm*) I don't think it is becoming of a man like . . .

DEFENCE: Did you, sir, reduce the volume of your radio set?

ARMITAGE: No. I didn't.

DEFENCE: Thank you. (*Pause*) Where were you on the night of the 31st January between 11.30 and midnight?

ARMITAGE: At the Police Station in Georgetown.

DEFENCE: Between eleven and eleven-thirty?

ARMITAGE: For the most part, in the Armitage School Staff Library.

DEFENCE: What do you mean by 'for the most part'?

ARMITAGE: Well, I left the library at about 11.25, went to my house discovered that my radio set had disappeared and made my way directly to the Police Station to report the matter.

DEFENCE: When you were in the Staff Library, and were joined by Mr Sambang Sambou, a member of your staff, were you still hearing the programme of Handel's *Messiah* that was in progress at your house?

ARMITAGE: (*Pompously*) We cannot bid the ear be still.

DEFENCE: (*Insisting*) Were you hearing it?

ARMITAGE: Of course I was.

DEFENCE: How far is the Armitage Staff Library from your house?

ARMITAGE: (*Thinking*) Well, about a hundred and fifty yards.

DEFENCE: Was anyone in your house when you left it for the library?

ARMITAGE: No. I was not going to make a long stay there.

DEFENCE: But you did, Mr Armitage. Did you lock your house with a key or make any attempt to secure your house from thieves?

ARMITAGE: There are no thieves in Georgetown (*Checking himself*), at least, I thought so until this unfortunate incident occurred.

DEFENCE: My dear sir, you are at liberty to think your thoughts, but what you said just now is not compatible with the facts. The empirical evidence available could substantiate a contrary view. Indeed, there have been thefts before this incident in your own staff compound when certain students from Yundum College were on teaching practice in March last year.

ARMITAGE: I'm sorry. I forgot about that.

DEFENCE: You left your house, then, for at least thirty minutes without locking it up; you did not leave anyone in the house, and your radio was pealing away apparently to no-one in particular but in actual fact to all your neighbours, who had their own individual radio sets, just as good as yours, and who were compelled to listen to your programme even at that late hour. You have already said you thought there were no thieves in Georgetown. Did you also think that by tuning your radio loud enough to be heard within a radius of over a hundred and fifty yards, you were doing some invaluable service to the community?

ARMITAGE: I certainly thought the neighbours would appreciate it.

DEFENCE: They didn't! That is all, my lord.

JUDGE: Are there any more witnesses to be summoned?

DEFENCE: None, my lord.

JUDGE: The Prosecution?

PROS: There is no need, my lord.

JUDGE: The Counsel for the Defence may wish to sum up the case in favour of the accused?

DEFENCE: My lord, I would require about half an hour to sort out my arguments.

JUDGE: The Court is adjourned for thirty minutes.

fx: Noises of chairs, voices, etc. Fade out

fx: Fade in voices, chairs, etc.

SERGEANT: Court, attention! Silence in court!

JUDGE: The Counsel for the Defence will now present his case.

DEFENCE: My lord, Members of the Jury, the case before us is, indeed, a very involved one. Legally, the charge may be dismissed quite simply. The accused is charged with stealing a Telefunken radio set belonging to the Principal of Armitage School, Mr Maxwell Armitage, which was sold to the latter by Messrs Tangalsahol Ltd. But the Prosecution has been singularly unsuccessful in demonstrating that the radio set that was removed from the plaintiff's house is identical with the one posted to him by Messrs Tangalsahol Ltd on 13th

September, last year. He has failed disastrously to show that
there is any theft involved in the matter. The number of the
set Mr Armitage claims is his is not the same which Messrs
Tangalsahol say they sold to him. (*Murmurs from court*)
Assuming, however, that the plaintiff was in possession of the
radio set now in the hands of the Police, the Prosecution has
not been able to show that this set was stolen by the accused
and not merely removed from the house of the said plaintiff
in accordance with the Laws of the Land, Vol. XXIII,
Chapter 13, Clause 25, which reads as follows:

> 'If a citizen is found in possession of firearms, musical
> instruments, radio and television sets, and other kindred
> manufactured articles that are subject to misuse; and if it
> can be proved that such a citizen has misused the
> firearms, musical instruments, radio or television sets or
> other kindred manufactured articles, to the annoyance
> of his neighbours or other groups of citizens, the article
> or articles so misused may be removed by the Police, a
> Member of the House of Representatives or a Justice of
> the Peace, with or without the owner's knowledge, and
> kept out of his or her reach and the matter reported to
> the nearest Police Station.' (*Pause*)

I would like Members of the Jury to note the sequence of
events as stipulated by Law and that the accused is a
Member of the House of Representatives. The moral
viewpoint hinges on the conflict between individual and
social rights. As an individual the plaintiff has every right to
possess a radio set and to make proper use of it. As a member
of society, however, he has an obligation to use his radio set
in such a way as not to disturb his neighbours or be a
nuisance to those who do not particularly wish to listen to
his choice of programmes. From the ethical point of view,
therefore, the plaintiff deserves to lose his set. Thus legally,
as well as morally, the accused, my client, cannot be
associated with the crime with which he has been charged.
My lord, Members of the Jury, the case for the defence rests
there.

Murmurs of approval

JUDGE: The Prosecution may reply.
PROS: My lord, Members of the Jury, we are not met to dispute

an ethical problem but a point of law. I have tried in my presentation of the case not to burden you with the irrelevant. There are two points, however, to which I would like to draw the attention of the Jury at this stage. First, it would appear that the two witnesses summoned by the Counsel for the Defence, as well as the accused himself, belong to the same political party, namely the Enlightened People's Congress. The plaintiff, though not a member of any one party in particular, sympathizes with some of the objectives of the Progress Party. It is not unreasonable, therefore, to suppose that the two witnesses planned or took part in the planning of the theft of the radio set belonging to the man who had refused an invitation to become a member of their party. Secondly, it is interesting to note the Defence Counsel's choice of witnesses. The first is obviously incapable of comprehending simple English, and appeared at certain stages in the course of his testimony to be almost certainly 'non compos mentis'. The political prejudices against the plaintiff were quite evident in the second witness. He struggled hard to create the impression that he had no ill-feelings against the plaintiff but, when pressed sufficiently, came out with the revealing fact that he loathed the political views of his immediate boss. My lord, Members of the Jury, need I say more?

Murmurs from the Court

JUDGE: Members of the Jury, you will retire in a few minutes to consider your verdict. But before you retire, it is my duty to remind you that it is now your task to consider in the light of the evidence before you whether or not the accused is guilty of the crime with which he is charged. Examine carefully the testimony of the witnesses. You must agree on your interpretation of the vital points. You will weigh and consider, according to Law, every statement that throws some light upon the case. You must be very careful how you distinguish between what is legal and what is moral. You will remember that the case at issue is primarily a point of law. You will have to decide for yourselves to what extent the moral issues have a bearing upon the legal aspects of the case. And finally, it is your duty, Members of the Jury, to return a verdict of 'guilty' if you are convinced beyond all reasonable doubt that the accused has committed the offence for which he is charged. You may now retire and consider your verdict. The Court is accordingly adjourned.

SERGEANT: Court, attention!

fx: Appropriate noises – retiring footsteps, chairs, voices, etc. – fade out

fx: Fade in court noises

SERGEANT: Court, attention! Court, attention!

JUDGE: The verdict of the Jury?

fx: Dead silence

FOREMAN: Not proven!

The silence continues, then suddenly there is a buzz of chattering

SERGEANT: Silence in Court! Silence in Court!

Silence once more

JUDGE: By the terms of the verdict, the accused is acquitted – but not absolutely. The Jury are not fully satisfied that he is innocent but are not, on the other hand, convinced that the evidence against the accused is overwhelming enough to prove his guilt. He is accordingly released with the warning that if fresh evidence is made available the case may be taken up again. The radio set will be returned to the plaintiff with this caution, that it is partly because the Jury is not fully persuaded that he is blameless that they have returned a verdict of 'Not Proven' against the accused. The Court is adjourned.

fx: Chattering

SERGEANT: Court adjourned!

fx: Voices and footsteps

Hold it!

fx: Crash as radio is dropped

C'BRIDGIA: It be for what reason?

SERGEANT: Where are you taking that radio set?

C'BRIDGIA: It is not for your business to interrupt the public beneficiary.

SERGEANT: The radio set you were taking away is the property of the Court. And anyway, you were a witness for the defence.

C'BRIDGIA: You have no intelligency knowledge. His Excellency the Judge says I am taking one to plaintiff.

SERGEANT: You will have to explain that to the Magistrate. I'm afraid you are under arrest.

C'BRIDGIA: You have no intelligency knowledge! You have no intelligency knowledge! Go let me! Go let me!

SERGEANT: Come along, my man – come along.

fx: Fade out

The Prisoner, the Judge and the Jailer

DERLENE CLEMS

Derlene Clems, *born in Accra in 1942, was educated there and in Koforidua. His plans for higher education were interrupted after a year at the University of Cape Coast. He has worked as a journalist and is now teaching. Apart from the play in this collection he has had two other plays broadcast in* African Theatre. *He is currently working on a novel and travels widely to other parts of West Africa collecting material for this and or plays and short stories.*

Recorded Sunday 17th January 1971

CAST
Prisoner – Bloke Modisane
Jailer – Rudolph Walker
Judge – Cosmo Pieterse

SOUND EFFECTS
Rain
Thunder
Passing lorry
Car approaching and stopping
Car horn

Scene: A desolate bus shed situated along a road in the heart of Accra
Time: Around midnight one night in 1967.

fx: It has been raining for some time now and the area is gradually
flooding. Few vehicles zoom past, splashing water and blowing their
horns. This continues intermittently till the flood makes the street
impassable in the course of the play

PRISONER: Seems like it's going to rain for ages.

JAILER: (*With nonchalance*) Mmm, ten years at least.

PRISONER: Ten years? You really believe that?

JAILER: (*Peremptorily*) Of course I do. I always say what I
believe.

PRISONER: And you want me to believe that, too?

JAILER: What . . . ?

PRISONER: About this rain lasting ten years . . .

JAILER: You don't have to if you don't want to. What's so very
strange about it, anyway?

PRISONER: (*Dreamily*) Oh, ten years seems so long a time;
almost a life time. I used to have a friend who was jailed
twenty-five years for murder but had to spend only ten in
prison.

JAILER: What happened? Was he released on parole?

PRISONER: No. He jumped jail.

JAILER: (*Getting excited*) Why, that's sensational. How did he do
it?

PRISONER: I was going to tell you how but I won't. Do you
think it's natural to discuss such matters with a fellow one
hardly knows?

JAILER: (*Judiciously*) Of course, you don't have to if . . .

PRISONER: We met for the first time in our bloody lives barely
an hour ago under this decomposed shed. Say . . . Who put
it up here?

JAILER: The City Council.

PRISONER: It wasn't here years ago. Why put it up?

JAILER: Why put it up . . . ? (*Holding his breath*) Why . . . it's for
for the benefit of would-be passengers on the Council's buses.

PRISONER: That makes it a bus stop, then?

JAILER: Yeah . . . but I thought you said something about being
a worker here in Accra?

PRISONER: I said so, but I've just been back after a long absence.
I was away in the north . . . the far north, you know.

JAILER: Is that a good reason why a fellow can't tell what a bus stop is?

PRISONER: In my days the bus stops were painted green . . . this one here is red. When did they change the colour, anyway?

JAILER: Nearly ten years ago.

PRISONER: (*With a start*) Why . . . everything seems to add up to ten years tonight. You've noticed it, of course?

JAILER: (*Yawning*) What . . . ?

PRISONER: The rain which is to last ten years . . . my friend who was in jail for ten years . . . and this colour which was changed nearly ten years, ago. (*Pauses and reflects*) Well, ten years or no ten years your . . . er, the Council folks don't seem to care a hoot about keeping this shed here in good order. Looks like it's going to crumble under the weight of this rain any moment.

JAILER: Yes, it will be down before the night is over.

PRISONER: And yet it's supposed to give us shelter for the next ten years . . . remember?

JAILER: Mm.

PRISONER: The City Council people should have thought of that before the rain began an hour ago. They should have known that this shed wouldn't survive another ten years.

JAILER: That's what I call inefficiency . . . but let's talk about something new. Those Council chaps don't interest me at all.

PRISONER: (*Compromising*) I was saying we hardly know each other although we've been trapped here under this rotten shed almost an hour, and it seems like it's going to rain forever . . . only it will last ten years, and not be everlasting.

JAILER: I'm going to introduce myself and hope you do the same. For all I know about you is that you used to have a friend who was jailed for murder but escaped after serving only ten years of his twenty-five year sentence.

PRISONER: That's right. You can tell me your name, now.

JAILER: It's Kofi.

PRISONER: Mine is Ama.

JAILER: You must be joking. (*The prisoner bursts out laughing*) Ama is a woman's name.

PRISONER: (*Between his laughter*) I'm glad you've appreciated the joke.

JAILER: Thanks for the compliment, but (*persisting*) tell me your name now that you know mine.

PRISONER: It's Ted! (*Matter-of-factly*) All the world calls me
   Ted.

JAILER: (*Doubtfully*) And this isn't another of your lies . . . I was
   going to say of your jokes.

PRISONER: (*In good humour*) No. You may call me Ted.

JAILER: And what do you do for . . . er . . . (*Finds it difficult to
   ask the question*) What do you do for a living?

PRISONER: (*Feigning surprise*) Well! You're very inquisitive . . .
   too inquisitive for my liking. What, for instance, has a man
   got to do with what another man does for a living . . . tell
   me?

JAILER: Perhaps I ought to have told you that I'm a journalist.
   My work is to write news . . . to write about people, that is.
   One needs to be as inquisitive, as they say, doing this sort of
   a job, you know.

PRISONER: (*Showing concern*) I hope you don't contemplate
   writing about me.

JAILER: Not if you don't want me to.

PRISONER: Well, I don't want you to. (*Sighs*) I'm a labourer
   with the Public Works Department.

JAILER: But I thought they'd changed the name to something
   like the State Construction Corporation. Do they keep the
   old name still, up there in the north?

PRISONER: No. Up there it's the S.C.C., of course, but formerly it
   was the P.W.D. My work is to construct the streets for the
   cars of the rich ones . . . the so-called 'big men'. And when
   I'm not building streets I may be found tilling the soil on the
   big plantations in the bush, but it's still the 'big men' who
   really enjoy the fruits of my labour. They own all the big
   plantations. They drain my strength for a song. Mine is a
   dirty job, I can tell you.

JAILER: Were you doing the same dirty job up there in the
   north?

PRISONER: (*Regretfully*) I was doing worse. They have the 'big
   men' up there in the far north too . . . sent there on transfer
   . . . and so I, too, had to be transferred there to dig gutters
   around their bungalows. And you know how much I got
   doing that? Five-and-six a day when I wasn't so sick as to
   absent myself from work.

JAILER: (*Pointedly*) Five-and-six a day makes only fifty-five
   pesewas, now.

PRISONER: Yeah, and I had to feed a wife and six children on it. Just you think of that! Feeding a wife and six children on only fifty-five pesewas. It's peanuts. Do you make something better by your writing?

JAILER: Yes. I make more than five times what you are making, but I have a wife and children, too, to feed.

PRISONER: How many children you've got?

JAILER: Two sons in college and a teenage daughter.

PRISONER: You don't have half my troubles, man. Yours is what I call a 'goody goody' life. You're just lucky.

JAILER: I suppose it is to you . . . but I wonder whether your friend is as unlucky as you.

PRISONER: Which friend do you mean?

JAILER: The one who was jailed for murder but escaped.

PRISONER: Man, you can be very curious when you choose, you know. Why are you so anxious to know about my friend?

JAILER: I told you I'm a journalist.

PRISONER: A very nosey type of a journalist.

JAILER: One has to stay that way if one is to succeed in my type of job, you know. Writing about people isn't all that easy, and so you'll have to excuse my curiosity.

PRISONER: (*Wanting to be sure*) You don't intend writing about my friend, though?

JAILER: No.

PRISONER: Then I'll tell you about him. He killed a man: his Boss to be exact, up there in the far north.

JAILER: (*Affirmatively*) Which means to say your friend wasn't lucky in his job, either.

PRISONER: That's correct.

JAILER: Do you think that's a good enough reason for a man to kill his Boss? It doesn't make sense to me.

PRISONER: It's true when I say that my friend wasn't lucky in his job, but had the Boss left him alone there wouldn't have been any murder either.

JAILER: So the Boss wouldn't leave your friend alone, eh?

PRISONER: Not for all the world!

JAILER: And so he killed him?

PRISONER: Mm.

JAILER: How did he do it?

PRISONER: He strangled him . . . squeezed his throat till his life ebbed away.

JAILER: Your friend must have the strength of a bull to do that kind of job . . . strangling a full-grown man.

PRISONER: I told you his job was to wield the pick and construct the roads for God knows which people. One can't help developing all the muscles which goes with that type of job, you know.

JAILER: I even dare say his hands might have been as broad as yours or mine to have killed that Boss in the fashion you talk of.

PRISONER: You're right. His hands were almost as broad as yours or mine, but we're forgetting something.

JAILER: What?

PRISONER: My hands and yours being broad, for example. The two of us are almost giants.

JAILER: I think I have the edge on you by at least four inches and besides I weigh two hundred and fifty pounds.

PRISONER: I'm six feet four inches tall. (*Pause*) Are you really six feet eight when you stretch your full height?

JAILER: Yes.

PRISONER: But the question is, which one could pack the heavier punches in a fight, if there is to be one?

JAILER: You don't have to doubt my strength if that's what is on your mind. I'm not only a giant . . . I can knock a horse groggy with just one blow . . . believe me!

PRISONER: That's some strength . . . but you haven't seen me in action yet. Why . . . I can knock out any heavyweight from here to Jericho.

JAILER: I'm inclined to believe anything that you tell me . . . but I think it will make sense to you if I tell you that I'm an expert in judo and karate.

PRISONER: (*Acknowledging defeat*) Why . . . man, you've almost had me cowered. You've made me as nervous as a stray dog.

JAILER: You don't need to be afraid of me, for in spite of my strength I'm as gentle as a lamb and as loving as a milk-maid. In fact, you needn't fear to tell me all about your friend and how he killed his Boss because he was treated badly.

fx: Thunder clap and the rain falls with renewed vigour

PRISONER: (*Avoiding talk of the murder*) The rain is falling in torrents, now. Seems like the whole place's in flood.

JAILER: Have you only just noticed it? The water began to mount about thirty minutes ago.

PRISONER: We've been here almost two hours, now.

JAILER: Two hours six minutes to be exact! My time says it is six minutes past midnight.

PRISONER: And the water is still mounting.

JAILER: There's hardly any rain in Accra without floods, nowadays. It all began just after independence . . .

PRISONER: (*Surprised*) So the Gold Coast now has independence.

JAILER: (*More surprised than the former*) But . . . but I thought you'd been in the country for the past ten years.

PRISONER: Yes.

JAILER: Then why do I have to tell you that the Gold Coast attained independent status as far back as nineteen fifty-seven and became Ghana?

PRISONER: You *are* telling me!

JAILER: (*Confusedly*) But you said you were in the north . . .

PRISONER: The far north to be exact . . . it makes a lot of difference, you know.

JAILER: How?

PRISONER: (*Weighing the words*) Living in the far north is like living outside the country. One hardly sees any papers one can read for news about what is going on in the country. One is simply cut off from the rest of . . . er, what did you say is the new name of the nation?

JAILER: Ghana.

PRISONER: Yeah . . . living in the far north is like living outside Ghana. You get no news about any self-government and independence. I would even say there's nothing like colonialism there . . . you just don't hear of it from anybody.

JAILER: (*With resignation*) Then I don't think it's great living in the far north.

PRISONER: I don't think so either. That way you never know what's going on down in the south. The country may blow to pieces without your having the slightest idea. So you just stay perched up comfortably there in the far north till the stench from the rotten mess of the country hits you right in the nose. Then it gets on your nerves . . .

JAILER: (*Astonished*) God! One can only behave like a beast when forced to a life like that. Take for instance your friend who killed his Boss . . .

PRISONER: (*Sharply*) I told you it was the Boss who wouldn't leave him alone.

JAILER: Yes . . . and added to those troubles there was the solitude and disquieting nature of the place. It's your friend who has my sympathy, not his victim.

PRISONER: (*Hesitating*) You sure you're not taking sides unreasonably?

JAILER: No. Your friend wasn't really responsible for the murder. I would say that he was driven by circumstances to do what he did.

PRISONER: (*Gratefully*) You are the first fellow in ten years . . . I mean the ten years since the murder . . . to hold this view. The Judge didn't, neither did the Jury.

JAILER: You were expecting the Judge to hold the same views as you?

PRISONER: I was expecting the best.

JAILER: But different people can only think differently!

PRISONER: Mmm.

JAILER: So the Judge and the Jury couldn't see things as we do now.

PRISONER: That makes us different people from the Judge and the Jury. (*Almost expectantly*) Say . . . are we the same people? I mean . . . same working-class type? (*Then realizing that to be impossible*) No, I don't think that is possible. I'm a poor labourer . . . son of another poor labourer. It has been so in our family ever since Adam and Eve were born. But look at your clothes. Look at your smart jacket and trousers . . . No, I'm a labourer and you're a journalist.

Pause

Where do you live?

JAILER: Here.

PRISONER: You mean here under this tottering shed?

JAILER: Of course! I used to have a home . . . or two . . . but for the next ten years this place is home whether I like it or not.

PRISONER: But where was your home before this rain started?

JAILER: Which of my homes?

PRISONER: (*Enviously*) So you have more than one, eh?

JAILER: I used to. There was my house at Tema which I shared with my sons and wife. There was that other one at

Koforidua where we spent our holidays . . . and then one or two flats where I can go right here in Accra. A journalist has to be that way, you know. (*Almost regretfully*) But now this place is my home.

PRISONER: For the next ten years, at least?

JAILER: Yes.

PRISONER: I'm staying here, too, for the next ten years but I don't hate it.

JAILER: Why?

PRISONER: (*Remorsefully*) Because I haven't got any place to go to.

JAILER: (*Shocked*) What . . . ? Where are your wife and children? Do they sleep under the open sky?

PRISONER: (*Caught unawares by the question*) Oh . . . my wife and children? (*Thinks fast*) Er . . . I left them in the north as a temporary measure. I couldn't bring them along since I've still got to find somewhere to live.

JAILER: How do you live, yourself? After toiling all day long in the field, where do you sleep?

PRISONER: I wish I could name a place, man!

fx: A truck passes very near, splashing water

JAILER: Good God!

PRISONER: God damn it! How that fellow in the truck nearly splashed us with muddy water. He took us to be a couple of rats, maybe.

JAILER: (*Sighs*) But soon there'll be an end to it. There's always an end to everything.

PRISONER: How . . . ?

JAILER: You don't know about the floods of Accra, do you?

PRISONER: No. What happens?

JAILER: Why . . . two years ago this particular area was flooded knee high, making the street impassable. It was like that for two days till the rain stopped. No lorries went by; not a single car could get through the water; and so for three days only a couple of canoes were used to ferry people across . . . even though it stopped raining . . .

PRISONER: But for the next ten years there'll be no ending to this rain: there'll be no ferries. You said it.

JAILER: Yes, I said it . . . and I believe it . . .

PRISONER: Which makes this place our home for the next ten years. We're going to stay together . . . we're going to be

neighbours right under this battered old shed of a bus stop.
You wait until the water gets a bit higher . . .

JAILER: Which is the more reason why we must get to know each other.

PRISONER: Oh . . . mmm. I was telling you about my friend who killed a man. That man was the Boss and so he took it upon himself to make another man suffer.

JAILER: What exactly did he do?

PRISONER: It will take days to tell you all the things he did. (*Pause*) Er . . . do you lose your pay for the day, when you arrive for work five or so minutes after the time-keeper has done his job?

JAILER: Which time-keeper?

PRISONER: What? Don't you know what a time-keeper is?

JAILER: Where I work we have no time-keepers!

PRISONER: Then you don't lose your pay either?

JAILER: No!

PRISONER: In our case we lost our pay even if we arrived only one minute past the bell . . . all five-and-six of it. And you know what followed?

JAILER: No! Not the slightest idea.

PRISONER: We were lucky if we didn't get sacked . . . but then the Boss made us work although we knew our pay was forfeit. That way we could keep the job if we still wanted to, but we were always deep in debt; and with our families starving there was no alternative.

JAILER: That was a primitive way of treating one's subordinates!

PRISONER: Oh, the Boss . . . he called it the 'art of self-discipline'. Fancy that toddler of a man trying to tell me about discipline. I was older than him by fifteen years and more.

JAILER: He was quite young, then?

PRISONER: He was not more than twenty-five; and straight from college. All the same he made us work while he took our pay.

JAILER: How did you know he took your pay?

PRISONER: (*Defiantly*) That was what sent him to his grave in the end! You remember what I said about this Boss cheating us?

JAILER: What did he do?

PRISONER: He made us work while he took our pay . . . but we didn't know at first he was doing it. As for me, I had to find a way out quick . . . because losing my five-and-six a day was like adding insult to injury.

JAILER: And how did you solve your problem?

PRISONER: It was simple. I was up and labouring in the trenches long before the sun's up in the sky . . . although the normal time was at eight.

JAILER: Well, couldn't your friend have . . .

PRISONER: He got his idea, too! A very plausible idea . . . only that it didn't work. He bought himself a clock and . . .

JAILER: You mean he bought himself a watch . . . a wrist-watch . . .

PRISONER: No, it was a clock . . . a table clock, he couldn't afford one of those wrist gadgets even if he'd wanted to. They cost much more.

JAILER: (*Facetiously*) So he bought himself a clock . . . an alarm clock, and carried it with him to work and back?

PRISONER: (*Eagerly*) Yes . . . he even learned to tell the time. Before then he couldn't tell three from four . . . but all the same his idea didn't work out.

JAILER: Why . . . ? I thought he carried his clock with him all day . . .

PRISONER: He did! At first we all thought his clock had developed some engine trouble. He got to work when his clock said it was thirty minutes past seven . . . only the time-keeper's clock wouldn't agree. When my friend's clock said it was seven-thirty that of the time-keeper said it was eight-thirty. When my friend got to work at quarter to eight the time-keeper said it was quarter to nine.

JAILER: Your friend couldn't have possibly learned to tell the time properly.

PRISONER: Yes he did! I wish you would listen to the end of the story.

JAILER: Sorry, go on.

PRISONER: As I was saying, my friend learned to tell the time very well and so he had great faith in his clock. He pitched all his hopes on the clock, and watched it carefully every day. (*Pauses for dramatic effect, then speaks with animation*) It was then that he made his great discovery . . .

JAILER: (*Impatiently*) Well, what was it?

PRISONER: He discovered that the time-keeper had been tampering with the official clock.

D

JAILER: What . . . ?

PRISONER: The Boss gave him the authority to do it so that they could make us work while they took our pay.

JAILER: What a terrible thing to do!

PRISONER: But the Boss . . . he called that the art of self-discipline. When I learned of it I was so shocked and afraid . . . but I stuck to my ways. I said to myself . . . Early to bed is early to rise, and be down in the trenches before the sun's up in the east. (*Sighs*) That way, I got my five-and-six each day without fuss.

JAILER: Your friend could have profited from your example . . .

PRISONER: (*Sharp and definite*) No! (*Matter of factly*) He had his own idea. Two people don't have to think the same way.

JAILER: No – but what happened?

PRISONER: He killed the Boss! Killed him in cold blood right in his own office. Four days before the murder they had a quarrel in that same office. You don't know my friend . . . he was a tough character.

JAILER: With arms as strong as steel?

PRISONER: Yes! He had a quarrel with the Boss which landed him in a police cell overnight. It was the Boss who should have been put in that cell . . . the cheating bastard. But even in death he belongs to those at the top of society; but how was my friend to know that since the Boss was at the top of society that put him above the law?

JAILER: That isn't an easy question.

PRISONER: So my friend got him four days later and broke his neck. They brought him down south for trial . . .

JAILER: Was it fair . . . the trial?

PRISONER: I won't say, for he lost and made an appeal and lost that, too. It was the colonial Governor who saved his life in the end. He was sentenced to hang on a tree . . . but the Governor made it a twenty-five year spell in jail.

JAILER: But he couldn't agree to the Governor's decision either?

PRISONER: No, so he jumped jail after serving only ten years of his sentence. I told you he was as tough as rawhide.

fx: A car approaches far off

Hey! (*Pauses*) Do you see what I see?

JAILER: What?

fx: Car horn

PRISONER: That car labouring through the flood. The water is almost knee high . . . do you think the driver can get through?

JAILER: We'll have to wait and see. Ehem . . . you were telling me about your friend and how he jumped jail.

PRISONER: Well, they were bringing him down to Accra. (*With animation*) They were transferring him from Nsawan to Ussher Fort when their car broke down. Before the Warders could say Jack Robinson he was up and tearing them apart . . . six men against one: it wasn't a fair fight, but I told you my friend was tough.

JAILER: He must be. I think that driver there is in trouble.

PRISONER: You told me an hour ago that when this place gets flooded the street becomes impassable.

JAILER: I don't think he'll get any further than this.

PRISONER: Well, he may as well join us here under this shed. That way there'll be three of us for the next ten years . . .

JAILER: Well, we won't get so lonely.

PRISONER: Look! The car is stopping, the bumper is almost submerged in the water. I think the flood has risen over knee-high now.

JAILER: The driver is getting down. Soon the car will be full of water . . . dirty water.

PRISONER: Listen! He is yelling something at us. I can't hear him through the rain.

JUDGE: (*Calls off mic*) Is there a gutter between me and you?

JAILER: What is he saying?

PRISONER: I can't hear him. He's got to come nearer.

JAILER: He is coming, now. He is wading through the water.

JUDGE: (*Calls nearer*) Is there a gutter between me and you?

JAILER: No. You can wade through and come to no harm.

PRISONER: Why . . . that fellow looks like somebody I knew way back.

JAILER: In the far north, probably?

PRISONER: Maybe.

JUDGE: (*Coming in on mic*) My clothes are soaked through (*Pauses*) Are you two waiting for a bus?

JAILER: No. There aren't any running now. Seems like we're trapped here for . . .

JUDGE: (*Recognizing someone he knows*) Oh, is that you? Mr Kofi of the *Sunday Telegraph*?

JAILER: (*Open-eyed*) Yes. Who do I have the honour of addressing?

JUDGE: I'm Baah of the Roxy Models. Some time ago you ran a story on my establishment, remember?

JAILER: Sure, sure! Mr Baah, the fashion designer. So glad to see you.

JUDGE: Glad to see you, too. How's business going?

JAILER: Not bad! Not bad at all. (*Slight pause*) Ahem . . . er . . . Mr Baah, meet my friend Mr Ted, a worker . . .

PRISONER: (*Correctively*) A labourer to be exact!

JAILER: Mr Ted works with the Public Works Department. He even thinks he knows you.

PRISONER: If you've been in the far north . . . that's where I lived most of my life.

JUDGE: I'm afraid I'm not the person . . . the fact is that I've never gone beyond Kumasi in my life. I'm glad to know you, though.

PRISONER: I'm also glad to know you, but you do look like the fellow I have in mind.

JUDGE: Do I? Well, what was he?

PRISONER: That's what I can't remember.

JUDGE: Well, I'm sure I'm not the person. A fellow can't forget about a fashion designer once they become acquainted, and that's what I've been all my life. Moreover I have to be in Accra all the time if I don't want to go bankrupt.

PRISONER: I see. Well, I must be mistaken.

JUDGE: Yes. How long have the two of you been here?

JAILER: Since the rain started.

JUDGE: I don't think it's going to stop yet.

PRISONER: No . . . my friend here thinks it's going to last ten years, and I agree.

JUDGE: Which means the three of us are making our homes here for the next ten years. The whole area is in flood. There's water stretching as far as the eye can see . . . I should have taken another road home to bed . . . that is, if I'd known the flood would last ten years . . . that way I wouldn't have had to sleep under open skies for a decade.

JAILER: We're not sleeping under open skies. We have this shed above our heads. In any case we all have our regrets, but we're trying to make the best out of it.

PRISONER: And, besides, we can't afford to have a solemn

neighbour sharing our lives for ten long years . . . one has to take life as it really is.

JUDGE: I'll do my best.

JAILER: Before you arrived, Mr Ted was telling me a story about a friend who killed a man . . . just a way of whiling away the time. Well, that friend of Mr Ted's killed a man . . . his Boss.

PRISONER: And was in prison for ten years . . .

JAILER: But he was actually sentenced to a twenty-five year spell. But the Boss brought about his own death. He was making it quite impossible for Ted's friend to live . . . so my sympathy is with the killer: not his victim!

JUDGE: But that is being sentimental. Why see things a killer's way? . . . all the same, human beings are sentimental creatures. You see . . . although the law found fault with Ted's friend, your sentimental mind makes you see things differently. I wish I knew about it so as to make my own judgment.

PRISONER: I'm wondering whether you can be trusted . . .

JAILER: I think we ought to trust him, since he is to share our lives for the next ten years.

PRISONER: I suppose we can't have a fellow we don't trust.

JAILER: And he has said that human beings are sentimental creatures . . . he is a human being, too, you see.

PRISONER: All right, I'll tell him the story. The Boss was making life not too pleasant for my friend . . .

JUDGE: So he killed him?

JAILER: He made Ted's friend work without pay. He was Boss and lord of the establishment . . . but Ted's friend couldn't leave his job because jobs were very scarce then.

JUDGE: But that isn't enough reason for a man to kill another man. There isn't much in it to win my sympathy. I mean . . . I don't see the point in your argument.

PRISONER: It's because you weren't there to see things for yourself.

JAILER: It's because you don't know what the life of a labourer really is.

JUDGE: True . . . I'm a fashion designer. I've been a fashion designer all my life . . .

PRISONER: Well, unlike you, I'm a labourer, and I've known the story of my friend at first hand. I knew about his suffering

children. I knew about his starvation and shame. He took me
home once to meet his family . . . and I won't ever forget
that experience.

JUDGE: Why?

JAILER: What happened?

PRISONER: The wife and two of his sons were in a room when
we got there . . . little boys they were, then. The rest . . .
two big boys and two big girls . . . were labouring somewhere
behind the house to make the barren soil yield food; but it
wasn't the rainy season nor harvest time. Just when we were
about to enter his compound the voices of the wife and the
two boys came to us. One son was crying and yelling to the
mother that he was hungry – none of them had eaten that
day. They were waiting for their father to bring them food
with the money he should have earned. He should have
earned five-and-six – it's not much, is it, for a whole day's
work? But rather that than have his family starve. Because
they did starve when he didn't get that five-and-six – and
often he didn't because of the Boss's cheating ways. That day
I went with my friend to his home the Boss had cheated him
again – he had no money, and no food. Imagine his feelings
as his children ran to us with so much hope and expectation!
Imagine how he felt as he saw their faces drop when they
saw he had nothing! (*Pause*) You know how they managed
to eat at all that night?

JUDGE: No.

JAILER: Go on.

PRISONER: I gave them a shilling from my own pocket to buy
food.

JUDGE: You've got a heart, only a few people this wide world
over would have done that.

JAILER: I maintain that this man was ill-used by that Boss
fellow . . .

JUDGE: Well . . . now that I know his story I'll say that your
friend has my sympathy, not his Boss.

PRISONER: This, then, is your judgment?

JUDGE: This is my own personal judgment . . . but the law can
see things its own way, you know.

PRISONER: (*Suddenly*) Look. Your car is drifting.

JUDGE: (*Not much concern*) Oh yes, the old crate is full of water,
and the water is still mounting.

JAILER: We're quite lucky that this shed has a high platform. We would have been waist-deep in water by now.

PRISONER: Why doesn't anybody do something about the flood, anyway?

JAILER: They've thought of it long ago!

JUDGE: They even dug a magnificent gutter . . . a sort of underground tunnel from the Kowley Lagoon area through the Odor quarters right down to the sea, but it didn't work.

JAILER: Then another fellow thought up a new idea, the lagoon must be dredged . . . fish and all . . . but although some engineers have been working on it for nearly three years now we don't know what's happened.

PRISONER: Meanwhile the flood is making things difficult for folks, see? And . . . (*Pause*) Hey, your car is still drifting away.

JUDGE: I'm not bothered. In fact, I won't be needing any car for the next ten years . . . this shed is home.

JAILER: What's more, we're not moving an inch from this place even if we want to, and so the car can drift its way to hell fire.

JUDGE: Yes, we shall be three trustworthy neighbours . . .

JAILER: (*Interrupting*) Three friends in need . . . to be exact!

PRISONER: For the next ten years . . . ?

JUDGE: Yes!

JAILER: (*Icily*) Yes!

PRISONER: (*Overjoyed*) In that case, gentlemen, I have something more to tell you.

JUDGE: (*Expectantly*) Yes?

JAILER: (*Much agitated*) Yes?

PRISONER: I want to make a confession.

JUDGE: Oh . . . sure. There's no harm in that.

JAILER: Besides it's good for the soul . . .

JUDGE: Yes, Ted . . . what's your confession?

PRISONER: I am my friend who killed the Boss!

JUDGE: What . . . ?

JAILER: What . . . ?

JUDGE: This is a riddle. It doesn't make any sense to me.

PRISONER: I mean I killed the Boss . . . killed him with my own hands!

JUDGE: Lord have mercy! You've made me shaky. I'm a-trembling like a leaf.

JAILER: Well that's a drastic confession to be sure.

PRISONER: But you needn't fear me.

JAILER: I don't fear you. I told you I'm as strong as three
man-killers.

fx: The rain dies down gradually

JUDGE: Well, both of you could match each other in a fair fight,
but me . . . I'll be neutral.

PRISONER: We're not going to fight . . . we've got to be good
neighbours for the next ten years, you know. (*Pause*) Why,
the rain's stopping.

JUDGE: . . . only to catch on again. That's how it rains,
nowadays.

PRISONER: And it's going to be like this for ten long years . . . ?

JAILER: Yes, but you were saying it was you who killed your
Boss. How does your friend come into the story, then?

PRISONER: He plays my role and I play his.

JAILER: Well, you made a good story out of it, didn't you?

PRISONER: I wanted to know if I could trust you first.

JUDGE: By all the mercies, your Boss made you suffer hell.

PRISONER: Mmmm, but I made him suffer more than he made
me.

JAILER: I suppose you did.

PRISONER: I wish you'd been there. (*Re-living the past*) Lord . . .
I can still see his face. How I made him scream!

JUDGE: (*Agape with expectation*) Go on, tell me.

PRISONER: The other workers were in the field when I got him.
The moment he saw me he knew something horrible was
going to happen. He was sitting behind his desk . . . furious,
beside himself as usual . . . yet when he saw me his
demeanour changed and he became quite modest and
friendly. He even got up to take my hand . . . you wouldn't
think he'd made me sleep in a police cell overnight a few
days before. He greeted me, even asked me to sit down. He
was scared out of his mind. I asked him if he was going to
stop his thieving and cheating. Then he started saying over
and over again what he'd do for me now, how he knew he'd
wronged me. You know he even offered to take me in on his
racket! All the time he was backing away, shaking with fear
and then as I went towards him he was begging, crying,

offering me all the money I wanted – It wasn't difficult – I got hold of him and I squeezed the life out of him!

JUDGE: Then you escaped after serving only ten years of your twenty-five year prison sentence?

PRISONER: Yes, they were bringing me to the Ussher Fort Prison for a change of air when I had my chance. I knocked my jailers out cold.

Pause

JAILER: (*Sighs*) Everybody knows about your escape, from here to Bawku. They ran a story on it in the papers three days ago with your pictures.

PRISONER: (*With boyish excitement*) Me in the papers . . . say, I'm famous then? I escaped nearly a week ago, and I've been making my home in secret places.

JUDGE: (*Serenely*) When I judged your case ten years ago I didn't have half the facts I have now.

PRISONER: (*Alarmed*) What do you mean by when you judged my case ten years ago?

JUDGE: Seems like we've got to make our own confessions, too . . . eh?

JAILER: Yes – well Ted, I'm not a journalist. In actual fact I'm a retired jailer . . . I retired only last year.

JUDGE: And I'm not a fashion designer. I'm a retired Judge of the High Court. I retired three years ago.

PRISONER: I thought I knew you the moment I saw you . . . how could I have forgotten your face? . . . you who gave me my death sentence.

JAILER: We happened to be driving along here when we saw you making for this shed . . . and what with the papers making all that noise about you . . .

JUDGE: And I think I got sort of excited because I was the very judge who sat on your case.

JAILER: In actual fact, we are twin brothers although we don't look alike. Seems to me like we were the type which develop from separate . . . what do they call it . . . ? So I happen to be a giant when my twin brother is nothing better than a dwarf.

JUDGE: Moreover, we happen to be connected with the law although we are retired men.

JAILER: And so I made a plot and concocted a story . . .

PRISONER: And see what it adds up to: a labourer prisoner at
the mercy of a judge and a jailer.

JAILER: Now I've told you that I am an expert in Karate
and . . .

PRISONER: I'm not going to fight you. There's no fight in me
now.

JUDGE: Well, then, (*imperatively*) come along! It's not raining now
and the water isn't a threat. We can wade through to the
nearest police station.

PRISONER: (*Pleading*) But we're supposed to be neighbours for the
next ten years.

JAILER: Come along, and don't try any tricks! I can knock you
out cold with just a blow.

PRISONER: But you said you understood – didn't you? (*Going off
mic slowly*) Please, we were going to be neighbours for the
next ten years – please, it will rain again – we were to be
neighbours – you said you understood.

fx: They wade away off mic through the water

Oh, how dearly I detest thee

JEANNE NGO LIBONDO

Jeanne Ngo Libondo, *born in 1946 in America, was educated there and took a B.A. in International Relations before becoming a Camerounian citizen on her marriage. She now lives in Douala, and in her spare time writes poems and children's books as well as plays. Another of her plays,* Joseph, haven't you got your bicycle yet, *has been published by Heinemann.*

Recorded Sunday 31st January 1971

CAST
Tambe – Alton Kumalo
Ako – Jumoke Debayo
Enoh – Paul Jacobs
Bessong– Lionel Ngakane
Arrey – Fred Ogunniyi
Villagers played by members of the cast

SOUND EFFECTS
Chair
Book
Box of books
Crockery
Door

Place: Tambe and Ako's house in a Camerounian village
Time: The present

*fx: A man opening and slamming a door, scraping his slippers loudly
across the floor, all the while whistling obnoxiously; then a woman
flings the covers angrily off a bed*

TAMBE: (*Sarcastically*) Good morning, wife.

AKO: (*Viciously*) And why would you, of all people, want to wish
me a good morning? You don't want me to have a good
morning; you were only trying to taunt me. Well (*Spits*),
hus-band, the same to you!

TAMBE: You are stupid beyond all imagination, Ako. Your
dressing-gown is on . . .

AKO: (*Victoriously*) Backwards! Just because you, my lord and
master, would prefer it otherwise.

TAMBE: Stop acting so senseless. Put it on properly.

AKO: Force me.

TAMBE: Oh, shut up. And when are you ever going to unpack all
these boxes piled up all over the room?

AKO: As soon as you paint these wretched, filthy walls.

TAMBE: I will not paint them until you wash them, and you have
continually refused to wash them.

AKO: That should not be my work. It would require a strong
man to wash them. Look how filthy they are!

TAMBE: I have told you to wash them. And that is that.

AKO: 'That' is most certainly not 'that'. You have commanded.
And I have refused. You cannot force me to do it.

TAMBE: I shall.

AKO: You are not man enough to force yourself to force me to do
anything, Tambe.

TAMBE: I am warning you, Ako, you had better wash those walls
today. Then I shall be most willing to buy the yellow paint
and paint the walls.

AKO: Blue!

TAMBE: Yellow!

AKO: Blue!

TAMBE: Yellow!

AKO: You see? Even if the walls were clean, you still couldn't
paint them, because you can't decide what colour!

TAMBE: *I* have decided. It's just your hardheadedness that you
want them blue. They will be yellow.

AKO: What difference does it make what you have decided? Whatever you decide, I will defy you, and you know that.

TAMBE: Enough of that, woman. Go fix breakfast, will you?

AKO: Whenever I am good and ready.

TAMBE: And then I want you to sew the buttons on my pyjamas. These ridiculous pins are beginning to make holes all over the place.

AKO: Not until you wash the walls, I won't.

TAMBE: But *you're* the one who's going to wash the walls. We already decided that.

AKO: (*Going off mic*) Then you will sew the buttons on your sacred pyjamas.

fx: Sounds of Ako's return, then noise of crockery being thrust on to a table. A chair scrapes as Tambe sits down

TAMBE: Why do you insist on bringing me porridge and coffee, porridge and coffee, porridge and coffee. You know full well that I like eggs and tea.

AKO: You have eaten porridge and coffee every morning since that blessed day three years ago when my father delivered me, kicking and screaming, to this your despicable house.

TAMBE: And every morning for three years I have asked you to bring me tea and eggs. Do you like porridge so much?

AKO: I detest it. But I eat it every day just for the pleasure of knowing it displeases you.

fx: Noise of rummaging in boxes

Where have you hidden my chemistry book?

TAMBE: If you would ever unpack those boxes you might just find it.

AKO: If you would ever paint the walls I might just unpack them.

TAMBE: If you would ever wash them I might just paint them.

AKO: *You* have got to wash them, I will not.

TAMBE: You must.

AKO: That's man's work.

TAMBE: That's woman's work.

AKO: That's man's work.

TAMBE: You just wash them like a good little girl, and then I'll paint the walls yellow.

AKO: Blue!

TAMBE: Yellow!

AKO: Blue!

TAMBE: Yellow!

AKO: Where did you put my chemistry book?

TAMBE: Why would an idiot like you want an old chemistry book?

AKO: I'm trying to see what usually ordinary household products have properties that could be – no. You just worry about it.

TAMBE: You wouldn't dare.

AKO: Oh, wouldn't I now? A routine accident – *such* a pity.

TAMBE: You need me too much to poison me.

AKO: Need what? Your fortunes?

TAMBE: Look, you're making me late for work again!

fx: Noise as Tambe jumps up from the chair and begins to go out.

AKO: (*After a moment*) Tambe!

TAMBE: (*Off mic*) No!

AKO: Come here!

TAMBE: (*Still off mic*) No!

AKO: (*Secretively*) All right, don't come.

TAMBE: (*Coming back on mic*) None of my shirts have buttons any more! There's not a single one remaining with all the buttons.

AKO: What a pity.

TAMBE: If you weren't such a lazy woman!

AKO: If you weren't such a lazy man – ! Oh, pardon me. I might say male of the species, but you are no man!

TAMBE: And you are no woman. Three years of marriage, and you still barren as a lava rock. I have a mind to send you back to your father.

AKO: You wouldn't dare! Because I would tell him *why* I have no child, and that is because my (*Shudders*) husband has never had the courage to consummate the marriage!

TAMBE: (*Defensively*) This marriage wasn't my idea.

AKO: Nor was it mine! But a man – I mean, a male – who can't bring himself to sleep with his wife, even after three years!

TAMBE: I should rape you for saying that, Ako, but the very sight of you fills me with such revulsion that the mere thought of touching you – see! I'm late for work, and still no shirt with all the buttons.

AKO: Today is Sunday, you idiot. That's what I was going to tell you a few minutes ago, but you were too obstinate to listen. There's no work today. Can't you even keep the days of the week straight?

TAMBE: Oh, no! A whole day with my charming helpmeet, my devoted, adoring wife!

AKO: That's fine. You will have plenty of time to wash those walls.

TAMBE: I am *not* washing those walls, for the seven hundredth time! I have directed you, ordered you, commanded you, to obey me for once in your miserable life, and wash those walls.

AKO: I will not.

TAMBE: Then I shall take you to the elders and tell them that in three years of marriage, never once have you obeyed me. And you know what they can do with disobedient wives. Especially women without issue.

AKO: (*After a moment's reflection, somewhat subdued.*) And I shall tell the elders that you are so weak, so impotent, that you have been unable to perform your masculine duty.

TAMBE: They would not believe you.

AKO: (*Smugly*) A simple examination would suffice.

TAMBE: (*After a moment's reflection*) But I should tell the elders how you have refused my advances. They will deal properly with you.

AKO: You would not, because that would only expose your own impotence.

fx: Rummaging in boxes

TAMBE: And you would not dare report me, because that should expose your incredible insubordination.

AKO: I still haven't found my chemistry book. I swear, if you would only wash those walls . . .

TAMBE: If you would only unpack those boxes . . .

AKO: If you would only paint the walls blue like I say . . .

TAMBE: Yellow!

AKO: Blue!

TAMBE: Yellow!

AKO: Ahah! Here's my chemistry book. Now, let me just find what I need.

TAMBE: You make me sick. Nothing but scheming all day long, from morning to night.

AKO: You never even bother to speak civilly to me; why should
    I be nice to you?

TAMBE: I'm going out. And when I come back I want those
    walls washed, and all the buttons on all my shirts, my
    pyjamas, and my trousers properly sewn on. Do you hear,
    Ako?

AKO: I have no ears for your orders. Besides, I have no thread.

TAMBE: How, no thread?

AKO: My miserly husband will not give me enough money to
    manage this so-called home properly, much less buy
    necessities like thread.

TAMBE: I give you far too much, and you squander it on things
    like . . . like . . . porridge.

AKO: For your information, porridge costs less than eggs. The
    way I have to stretch things in this house to make ends
    meet . . .

TAMBE: Oh, shut your mutinous mouth, you wretch.

AKO: And who are you to tell me what to do?

TAMBE: I am your husband, whom you are bound to obey.

AKO: And I am your wife, to whom you are bound to at least
    attempt to give children.

TAMBE: How could I inflict upon any innocent child the horror
    of having you for his mother?

AKO: And how I would pity him who has a rotten piece of straw
    like you for a father!

TAMBE: You have no capacity for pity within you.

AKO: And you – you simply have no capacity for anything!

TAMBE: I am leaving, I said, going out. And I want all those
    buttons sewn on when I come back.

AKO: Without thread?

TAMBE: Without thread – with thread – but I'm not giving you
    a penny.

AKO: First of all you tell me to do something, then you make it
    impossible for me to do it, then you blame me when it
    doesn't get done.

TAMBE: Oh, shut up.

fx: Leafing through book

AKO: Oh, I'm not sure this book will help me anyway. I think
    what I need is a first-aid book. They always have a list of

antidotes for household poisons . . . Do we have a first-aid book? It runs in my mind . . .

TAMBE: You need me, Ako. You could not poison me because you need me to hate. Everyone needs someone to hate.

AKO: I don't hate you, Tambe. I *loathe* you, I *despise* you, I *abhor* you.

TAMBE: You have been threatening to murder me for three years. First, you said you would strangle me when I was sleeping. Then it was going to be suffocation. Now it's poison. But your threats are all meaningless, and you know it just as well as I do.

AKO: One of these mornings when you wake up dead, then you'll believe me. I think we do have a first-aid book.

fx: Rummaging through boxes

TAMBE: When are you ever going to unpack those cartons? For three years they've been sitting there, and you are too lazy to unpack them.

AKO: Lazy! Who's lazy? For three years you haven't lifted even a finger to paint those hideous walls.

TAMBE: Because you haven't washed them.

AKO: I am *not* going to wash those walls, especially when you refuse to even paint them a decent colour. Ahah! Here's the first-aid book. Now, where is that part about poisons? Ahah! A whole huge list of them, in alphabetical order. And to think we even have some of them around. Bleach . . . rat poison . . . roach powder . . . You see, Tambe? You had better start worrying.

fx: Sound of knocking

TAMBE: (*Lowering his voice*) You open it!
AKO: Never. You.

fx: Door opens

TAMBE: (*Off mic, pleasantly*) Oh! Come in!
ENOH: Hello, Tambe.

fx: Door shuts

AKO: Oh, hello, nkwane. Welcome. How are you? Won't you come in and sit down?

TAMBE: Nkwane, welcome.

ENOH: (*Coming on mic*) Nkwane, ngone, good morning. I am quite well.

TAMBE: (*Coming on mic*) Sit down, Enoh. What would you like to drink?

ENOH: Oh, I can't take anything now, thanks. I just stopped by to tell you something.

AKO: (*Going off mic*) Oh, Enoh, you really must take something. (*Shouts*) How about a bit of palm-wine?

ENOH: Oh, no thanks. Ako, really.

AKO: (*Coming on mic*) Just a half a glass, okay?

fx: Wine poured

There.

ENOH: Well, all right, thank you.

TAMBE: So, what is it?

ENOH: Chief Bessong's eldest son is coming back from the States tomorrow on the 1.15 plane. He has his master's degree in geology, you know, and some American oil company has already kept a big job aside for him in Douala.

TAMBE: So he's finally coming back, after all these years. What – six years since he's been away.

AKO: Yes, something like that. He had already been gone for a couple of years before Tambe and I got married.

TAMBE: (*Sarcastically*) Oh, blessed day. (*Catching himself*) So, David is coming back tomorrow.

ENOH: We're going to meet at Arrey's house at 12.30 and all go to the airport together to meet him. Then we'll go to the Chief's house; there'll be a big celebration.

AKO: Is he bringing his wife? I hear he married an American – a Southerner, even. A white girl.

ENOH: Yeah. David must be something, eh? But he would have been such a good match for one of our own girls. My father even tried to arrange a marriage for him with my junior sister, but David wouldn't hear of it. He said arranged marriages were a thing of the past.

TAMBE: (*With only a touch of bitterness*) But that's our tradition. What's wrong with arranged marriages? Look at our own, for instance. Three years so far, and still going strong. (*Coughs*).

AKO: You didn't say whether or not he was bringing his wife.

ENOH: Oh, I'm sorry. She's staying on in the States for a few more months to finish up her degrees.

TAMBE: What? She's even a graduate. David must have really done some charming.

ENOH: Well, sorry to rush off, but I've got to tell the others. See you tomorrow, Tambe.

AKO: (*Protesting*) I'll see you, too.

TAMBE: Male affair.

ENOH: You women will get your chance when the wife comes.

AKO: That's not fair. We just cook, and you men just gorge yourselves.

ENOH: (*Laughing*) Male affair, no females allowed. If you go, Chief Bessong will fine you a goat for sure. (*Going off mic*) Okay, now, I've got to go.

TAMBE: (*Going off mic*) Thanks a lot for coming by, Enoh. See you, what time?

fx: Door opens

ENOH: 12.30, Arrey's house.

TAMBE: Fine. Thanks, nkwane.

ENOH: Nkwane, ngone, good bye.

AKO: Nkwane, good bye.

TAMBE: See you tomorrow.

fx: Door closes

TAMBE: (*Coming on mic, victoriously*) Hah! So you don't get to go. Only us men.

AKO: There you go again, calling yourself a man. You are an affront to the masculine race.

TAMBE: I say, my loving wife, I'm going out.

AKO: Where are you going?

TAMBE: Maybe I'll go to the chemist and buy us some poison, because I have my own ideas, too, you know. I just haven't been stupid enough to broadcast them to you. If I could think of a way to remove you from this world 'accidentally', I'm sure I'd get some sort of prize from humanitarians. Maybe even the Nobel Peace Prize.

AKO: You wouldn't murder me for the same reason I can't murder you. If there's one thing to say for our marriage, it's that we're equally matched. You hate the sight of me no

less than I hate the sight of you. Now I repeat: where are
you going?

TAMBE: (*Mockingly*) Maybe I'm going to see my girl friend.

AKO: That's a laugh! You, who can't even bring yourself to
sleep in the same bedroom with your wife!

TAMBE: Maybe that's why I'm going to see my girl friend.
Maybe my wife is so ugly and so repulsive that I *need* a girl
friend.

AKO: You are boasting for nothing. You aren't even man enough
to have a girl friend. All right. You go see your so-called girl
friend; I'll go see my boy friend while you're out.

TAMBE: Hah! Is that ever a laugh! First you insist you're still a
virgin, then you claim to have a boy friend. In any case, I'm
going out. Goodbye.

AKO: You wouldn't have the faintest notion of whether I was still
a virgin or not. Goodbye, and good riddance. Don't forget
my thread.

TAMBE: (*Going off mic*) Blast your thread!

fx: Door opens

AKO: Blast you!

fx: Door slams shut

Blast your ugly face, Tambe. Blast every wretched thing
about you. Oh, what a miserable life with that man. Oh!
How our parents could have been so cruel as to force us into
marriage, I'll never know. I'll never do anything like that to
my children . . . my children. My children who will never
be . . . Not to say that I really want any from that hyena of
a husband of mine. Grr – I so detest him. I wish I could just
arrange some way to get rid of him neatly, quietly, quickly.
(*Short pause*) But then what would I do? Whoever would
want a woman who has been married for three years
without a child? But there again, why should I have to
remarry anyway? I can go to a trade school – learn
secretaryship – get a job – support myself instead of always
being at the mercy of someone else. I think I'll just wait for
the proper moment. We have all sorts of things in this house
which I could use, really . . . there are mushrooms, sleeping
pills, rat poison which I could mix with the sugar real strong
to put on his porridge. In fact, while I'm thinking about it,

let me just mix some of that rat poison with the sugar. It might take a few days to take effect, but that would be even better than a sudden death. I would have left him ages ago except for the embarrassment of being a married virgin. And he would have sent me packing long ago too except out of fear of having his own weakness exposed to public view. What sort of insane life is this? A marriage based on hatred and mutual embarrassment. It is so intolerable; something has just got to happen. I've waited for three years, but I don't think I can wait any longer. Let me go fix up that sugar . . .

Fade out

Fade in •

TAMBE: (*Yawning, whistling the same obnoxious tune as before, scraping his slippers as annoyingly as possible*) Good morning, Ako.

AKO: *Must* you always whistle that same old tune?

TAMBE: I have the right to whistle whatever I want. You never have sewed the buttons on my pyjamas. How many times have I told you?

AKO: You just went out yesterday, but do you think you could remember to bring me thread? No, not Tambe. He would just prefer to have something to complain about.

TAMBE: I have given you plenty of money to buy hundreds of reels of thread. But you squander it away on . . . on . . .

AKO: Things like food. You never will understand how much food costs in this place. You complain that the meat I buy is tough . . .

TAMBE: Oh, shut up. Look, this afternoon I'm going out to the airport to meet David Bessong. I haven't a single shirt with all the buttons. You know, Ako, that is a very bad reflection on you. A wife is supposed to take reasonably good care of her husband's clothes.

AKO: Naturally. But husbands are also supposed to make it possible for their wives to buy extra buttons and thread.

TAMBE: Enough! (*Scrapes across the floor off mic, whistling, then returns as Ako speaks*)

AKO: You and that whistling! I often think the next time I hear that song I'll just go round the bend.

TAMBE: That would be great. Then they could lock you up somewhere and everybody would forget about you. (*Whistles with renewed vigour*)

AKO: Grrr!

TAMBE: Here! Here's your thread! I brought it yesterday, in case you're interested.

AKO: (*Shocked*) What? *You* actually condescended to buy *thread*? (*Laughs viciously*) Now you can sew your buttons on.

TAMBE: (*Coolly*) Now look, Ako. For once in your life I want you to listen to me. I am going to the airport this afternoon to receive David Bessong. David is a big man now, and I don't want him to think I'm doing so badly I can't even afford to have my clothes mended properly.

AKO: In other words, you don't want him to know what a failure, what an absolute flop, you really are.

TAMBE: You can't ever stop arguing, can you? Now look. I brought the thread. Here are some buttons. Now you sit down and you fix at least one shirt. Is that so unreasonable?

AKO: Force me.

TAMBE: I ask you, is that so unreasonable?

AKO: Do it yourself.

TAMBE: You want David Bessong to know that you are so lazy, so disobedient, that you won't even sew buttons on your master's shirt?

AKO: There you go again with this 'master' foolishness. I say, do it yourself.

TAMBE: (*Self-righteously*) All right, Ako. I will sew them on myself. Now get me breakfast immediately. Look, I'll be late for work again.

AKO: It's nearly ready. Everything but the sugar. I don't think I've made the rat poison concentrated enough yet. I'll give you plain sugar this morning, but from tomorrow, you'd better be careful.

TAMBE: Oh, you and your empty threats.

AKO: You shouldn't be so sure about that, Tambe.

TAMBE: Just get breakfast like a good little girl, while I sew on these buttons. I won't be home for lunch, remember; I'll be at Chief Bessong's house.

AKO: So much the better. At least I can have one peaceful mealtime in this house.

TAMBE: There! All sewed on! You see? That wasn't such a

traumatic experience. You could have done it yourself with a tenth of the effort you've spent complaining and refusing to do it.

AKO: Big deal.

TAMBE: Look, Ako, I know you won't believe me, but I sewed these buttons on to protect you and your reputation. Can't you see that? I don't want David Bessong to think that you're the lousy wife you really are.

AKO: Just because he'd figure out from that that you're a lousy husband.

TAMBE: Oh, shut up.

AKO: Shut up yourself, you big lout.

TAMBE: (*Going off mic*) Okay, I'm nearly late. No time for your lousy breakfast now. See you tonight.

AKO: Say hello to David for me.

fx: Door opens

TAMBE: Oh, get lost.

fx: Door slams

Fade in

fx: Door knocking

AKO: Who could that be? (*Going off mic*) I thought everyone would be at Chief Bessong's house. Yes?

fx: Door opens

Why! Chief Bessong! Welcome, welcome. (*Joyfully*) What a surprise. Nkwane, welcome. How are things? And Enoh, and Arrey. Welcome all. Come in, come in. (*There is heavy silence*) Please sit down. (*Pause*) Where's Tambe? What's the matter? (*Clearing of throats and shuffling of feet*) Someone tell me, what has happened?

BESSONG: Ako, there has been something of an accident.

AKO: Chief, chief! What has happened to Tambe?

BESSONG: We all went to the airport to collect my son David.

AKO: (*Impatiently*) Yes, yes . . .

ENOH: And on the way back . . .

ARREY: Let the chief speak, nkwane.

BESSONG: . . . On the way back, Arrey's car has a flat tyre, there near the cliff where there's no good place to get off the road to change it. Tambe offered to help fix it, and while he was in the middle of the road removing the flat, a huge lumber truck came at a very great speed, and . . . (*his voice breaks*)

AKO: (*Gasping in horror*) . . . and . . . ?

BESSONG: He was dead before we even got him to the hospital.

AKO: Dead! Tambe dead! Oh, my God! (*Begins to sob convulsively*)

ARREY: We're all so sorry, Ako.

BESSONG: Asya, ngone.

ENOH: Asya, Ako.

AKO: Where is he? Oh, Tambe, Tambe!

BESSONG: They're bringing the corpse here, ngone. We will bury him tomorrow.

AKO: Tambe, a corpse. Oh, Tambe, how? Oh, God.

BESSONG: You can all go. I want to see Ako alone for a few minutes.

The others depart, repeating 'asya' several times. Ako is sobbing softly

fx: Door shuts

Now, Ako. I know your marriage was not the most exemplary, nor was it the happiest: for three years you have not been blessed with a single child. You are lucky that Tambe was as kind as he was; many men put away their wives if they remain barren after even two years.

AKO: But –

BESSONG: (*Gently*) Listen, my daughter. Children are so important to us, you know that. Now, under very tragic circumstances, to be sure, your marriage to Tambe has come to an end. A childless marriage, completely without issue. That is a very, very grave matter.

AKO: (*Whispering*) Tambe, Tambe.

BESSONG: A very serious matter indeed. Now you know what our custom is under such circumstances. Tambe has two brothers. There is Solomon Abi, of course, and Benjamin Takor. You will of course be free to choose which, but you must decide whether it will be with Solomon or Benjamin that you will base your dead husband's children. Benjamin is the elder; unless you object we will presume that you accept him.

AKO: Tambe, Tambe.

BESSONG: My daughter. I know you are quite distraught at the moment. We are all deeply touched by this tragedy which has entered into our very bones. I will not force you to decide immediately. But you must continue the lineage.

AKO: (*Numbly*) Yes, chief, yes; the lineage must be continued.

fx: Knock on door, pause, then door opens. Several men can be heard carrying a heavy object

BESSONG: Tambe has come home, my daughter.

AKO: (*Sobbing*) Oh, Tambe, my Tambe, Tambe.

BESSONG: Lay him on the couch.

fx: Feet shuffle. The body is laid out; the men say 'asya, ngone', and exit

We will leave you alone with your grief, Ako. You will have time to reflect, ngone, time to decide between Benjamin and Solomon. Asya, my daughter, asya.

AKO: (*Weakly*) Thank you, chief, thank you. You are very kind to come yourself, nfor, very kind.

BESSONG: Asya, my daughter. (*Going off mic*) May the ancestors guide your thoughts and give you strength.

AKO: Thank you, chief.

fx: Door closes. Ako is alone with Tambe's body. There is the sound of Ako's soft sobbing, which abruptly stops

AKO: Tambe, Tambe! Enough of this sickening play-acting; everyone's gone. What a relief to see you spread out there quiet for once and for all! Now no-one can blame me for what I wanted done all along – a nice, clean, quick, accidental death. (*Laughing victoriously*) Oh hoh! (*Pause*) But wait a minute. What am I going to do about this custom of wife-inheritance? I never thought about that before. (*With real alarm*) Oh, Tambe, look what you've gone and done! I don't want to belong to either one of your stupid brothers just for the privilege of having children I was supposed to have from you. But if I refuse to accept one of them, then the family would be sure to ostracize me and I wouldn't have any way to live. Oh brilliant thinking, Tambe. Congratulations. It looks like you have won at last. (*Pause*) Don't just lie there staring into eternity, you big lout! Say something! Argue!

Threaten me! Do something! Don't just lie there as if you
were . . . dead.

Tambe, Tambe! (*Sobs*) Why aren't you arguing with me?
Why aren't you threatening me, why aren't you shouting at
me? I can't bear this silence, this . . . deathly . . . silence. I
can't stand being alone like this, Tambe, I just can't stand
it! It was such a comfort, knowing you would come home
every night, so reliably, so that we could fight. I felt so secure
in this awful little house. I used to derive so much pleasure
from trying to see which one of us could make the other
more miserable. (*Pauses, speaks brokenly*) But now you're gone,
Tambe. I won't ever hear you whistle that dreadful song of
yours again. Oh, Tambe, Tambe. How miserable I must
have made these last three years of your life! What a
wretched, wretched wife I've been. Three years – and never
once have we been to bed together. Incredible! I know you
detested me, Tambe, but really, you should have at least
tried. I know too that I am not the most provocative and
beautiful of women in this town, but, after all, I was your
wife, and you had that duty which you, in all your weakness,
could never bring yourself to perform. (*Short pause*) But there
again, it wasn't really all your fault. The first few times when
you did make your advances I turned you away so savagely
that you just sort of gave up. But now, three years later, here
I am, still a virgin, and now Chief Bessong wants to give me
to one of your brothers to continue the line! How could I
ever face either of those two men in this condition? Oh,
Tambe, Tambe! See what a fix you've left me in! But how
am I going to expose your own weakness like that to your
brothers?

Benjamin really isn't such a bad sort of fellow, but he's
getting a bit modern and I don't think he would very much
like the idea of having another wife, especially one like me.
Solomon is fast becoming an alcoholic.

He doesn't even take care of the wife he does have – he'd
never do anything for me at all. And he is such a loud-mouth
that I'm sure he'd broadcast the fact that I'm still a virgin
to everybody in town.

Oh, Tambe! See what a dreadful position I'm in? Benjamin
wouldn't want to take me I'm sure, I can't bear the thought
of going with Solomon, and in any case I couldn't face the

humiliation of exposing my true self to them. Oh Tambe, and to think that I was going to poison you tomorrow! Or was I, really? I wanted to get rid of you, I know, but at the same time – at the same time – I *needed* you, Tambe. Oh, Tambe, I feel so deserted, so alone! What really am I going to do? No matter what I do, I either expose both our weaknesses or have no means of support. And for some odd reason I don't want you to be disgraced now that you are dead. Why am I so worried about being fair to you now? I am supposed to have hated you. Why do I feel concerned that you can't defend yourself now? Why don't I feel happy any more that you're dead? Why do I feel miserable, in fact, now that you're not here? Why don't I want to bring shame to your memory? Why do I feel myself becoming almost . . . it's as if I feel *loyal* to you, Tambe. (*Thoughtfully, gently*) I just don't understand anything any more. I am afraid of facing life without you, Tambe, in fact absolutely terrified of what is to come. No matter what I do I will be humiliated myself and bring shame on to you. Oh, Tambe, my poor dead Tambe. I just can't seem to face life without you beside me. Unless . . . unless . . . oh, no. But there again, why not? That way I wouldn't have to go to either Benjamin or Solomon. I wouldn't have to confirm to everyone what a wretched wife I've been, and above all, Tambe, I would not have to shame you. I would not bring disgrace on to you, my poor dead husband. And I would not have to face life without you.

But what a dreadful thing to do, to take one's own life. How really miserable I must be, to even contemplate such a thing. But I must ask myself if I would be less miserable, living out the rest of my life in disgrace, and at the same time being the cause of everlasting shame on your name, Tambe. No. (*Going off mic*) I could not betray you now. (*Pause*) (*Coming in on mic slowly*) There it is, Tambe, the rat poison I was going to put on your porridge. (*Softly*) Well, your worries are over, Tambe, and mine soon will be too. Oh, God, how am I supposed to get this wretched stuff down? It smells awful, and I think I'll probably have to take the whole box of these tablets in order to make sure it really works. I don't think I could chew them; (*Going off mic*) I guess I'd better get some water. (*Pause*) (*Coming in on mic slowly*) All right, Tambe, I'm ready. (*Takes a deep breath and gulps down the poison, coughing and spluttering*) Ooooh, I surely didn't pick a very pleasant way to leave this world. Tambe, my Tambe – (*Her voice is growing weaker*) let me hold your cold hand, my husband. Let me . . . let me . . . kiss your life-less l-ip-s, my be-lov-ed.

Lagos, Yes, Lagos

YEMI AJIBADE

Yemi Ajibade, *born in 1935, was educated at Abeokuta before going to London where he studied acting and directing at* The Actors' Workshop *and then film making at the* London Film School. *He has appeared in many roles in films, on television and on the stage (including Nelson Mandela in* South Africa 70) *and taken many leading parts in* African Theatre *productions. Amongst other plays, he directed, in 1966,* Wind Versus Polygamy *for the First Festival of Negro Arts in Senegal. This is the first of his plays to be published, but others have been performed both in Britain and in France.*

Recorded Sunday 23rd May 1971

CAST	SOUND EFFECTS
Mugun Yaro – Gordon Tialobi	*Cock crowing*
Baba Osa – Bloke Modisane	*Door with lock*
Josiah – Willie Jonah	*Large rattle*
Mama Taiye – Carlien Bartels	*Bicycle bell*
Mama Adisa – Jeillo Edwards	*Market crowd*
Taiye – Annie Domingo	*Coins and paper money*
Awanatu – Taiwo Ajai	*Wooden chest*
Corporal Layi – Kwesi Kay	*Crockery*
Sergeant Momo – Cosmo Pieterse	*Whistle*
	Handcuffs jingle and clink

Place: Ofi, a small town surrounded by small villages half-way between
    Lagos and Abeokuta in Nigeria
Time: July 1944 – market day

fx: Cock crows – early morning. Baba Osa is snoring away in the nearby
    room. Mugun opens door, the snoring becomes heavier

MUGUN YARO: (*Coming in on mic*) Wake up master! The cock has
    crowed.
BABA OSA: Hun . . . Her . . . go away (*Goes back to sleep – he*
    begins to snore again)
MUGUN YARO: Master, the cock has crowed, wake up, master!!
BABA OSA: Hum . . . Hum . . . What? The cock! Eh! eh!
    (*Stretches and yawns*) Ah good lad.
MUGUN YARO: The cock has just crowed.
BABA OSA: O.K. I heard you. Where is Josiah?
MUGUN YARO: I don't know sir. I just wake up myself.
BABA OSA: Never mind. Maybe he's gone to shit in the nearby
    thicket. But I warned him not to go out in this town after
    dark or before daylight. Well! Mugun Yaro, go and get
    water ready for me to bathe.
MUGUN YARO: Sir, I discovered too late last night that the water
    had nearly finished in the jar.
BABA OSA: What! You mean there is no water for me to bathe
    with, and you and I slept under the same roof? You block-
    head! Come closer.
MUGUN YARO: Sorry, sir, I beg, it will never happen again. I was
    too busy roasting the chickens for supper last night. I beg,
    sir!
BABA OSA: Come closer, I say.

fx: A slap and a kick and a punch

MUGUN YARO: Yea! Yea! (*Wails in agony as he tumbles and rolls on*
    the floor)
BABA OSA: Shut up! You son of a coward. How many times have
    I warned you not to make that horrible noise when I hit
    you? (*He hits again*)
MUGUN YARO: I have stopped, sir! (*Trying to suppress his pain*)
BABA OSA: You! (*As he delivers four more thudding blows. Mugun*
    grunts heavily as each lands) That's right now. Never forget
    your discipline!

MUGUN YARO: No, sir, I will never forget it.

BABA OSA: Go immediately to catch one of those early water hawkers. Away, before I smash your wooden skull.

MUGUN YARO: (*Going off mic quickly*) Yes sir! Sorry, Junior Master!

JOSIAH: (*Off mic*) Eh! Mugun, what's the matter?

fx: Door closes

Hey, Baba Osa. What's the matter with him?

BABA OSA: Everything is O.K. Just a bit of timely correction. Where have you been so early in the morning, Josiah?

JOSIAH: I just took a stroll round in the neighbourhood.

BABA OSA: Listen, and listen carefully. You are my guest. I know this town, and I warned you when you arrived to keep off the streets at all dark hours. You know as well as I do why we have to have eyes that can see.

JOSIAH: Okay, I'm sorry.

BABA OSA: Good! Now it's getting late. Go on to the veranda for a minute while I do my supplication.

JOSIAH: (*Going off mic*) O.K.

fx: Door opens and closes

BABA OSA: (*In a solemn and deliberate sing-song*) Earth! Earth!! Earth!!

fx: Shake of some object that produces a sound like some giant box full of matches each time he says 'earth'

BABA OSA: I call you;
Do not call me back in a hurry.
Keep me and feed me
That I may not die young,
That I may not grow old into poverty.
Earth! you are the mother of the market;
Sons trample on you arrogantly, slaves march on your surface rudely.
You can be kind; you can be cruel.
You first feed children of man;
You then feed on man and his children.
(*Object shaken violently, as if he is possessed*)
Be with me today.

Whatever I do in the market today, I do.
Witches of the market are my mothers.
Wizards of the market are my fathers.
Albinos never see properly in daylight;
May they never see me properly,
During all our operations today. So be it. Ah!

fx: Object shaken three times

Pause

fx: Knocks on door. Door opens

JOSIAH: (*Coming in on mic*) Is it all right to come in now? Mugun
   Yaro is back.

BABA OSA: Come right in, Josiah. We must get ready
   immediately now. I have a great feeling it is going to be a
   prosperous market. (*Shouts suddenly*) Mugun Yaro!

MUGUN YARO: Sir, the water is ready for you, sir.

BABA OSA: You see, that boy can be fantastic after he's had his
   dose. He is like a racehorse – always needing whipping for
   top performance. (*Pause*) What's the matter, Josiah? You
   look worried.

JOSIAH: I'm O.K. Nothing really is the matter. I just wonder
   about life sometimes.

BABA OSA: Don't wonder about it. Live. That's my style to it.
   O.K., I'll have a quick wash down and back with you in a
   minute . . . oh . . . yes . . . (*Stops*) if you want some hot pap
   and bean-cake, Mugun Yaro will see to it. I always leave
   some money on him as petty cash. (*Shouts*) Mugun Yaro!

fx: Door flung open

MUGUN YARO: (*Running on mic*) Sir!

BABA OSA: Josiah will tell you what he wants. And fill your own
   belly too. I don't want anything. (*Hums a light cheerful
   African tune as he goes off mic*)

MUGUN YARO: Junior Master, how much pap and bean-cake
   would you like, sir?

JOSIAH: No, I don't want anything to eat. You may get yourself
   something. Just get me two sticks of cigarette, Bandmaster or
   Guinea Gold brand.

MUGUN YARO: Yes, sir. (*Runs out*)

JOSIAH: Hey, don't rush – it's not life or death! That boy is
   incredible . . .

Fade out

Fade in

MUGUN YARO: Here, Junior Master. A whole tinful of
  Bandmaster cigarettes – (*Proudly*) an unopened one too, sir.
JOSIAH: A whole tin of fifty! I said two sticks of cigarette!
MUGUN YARO: I heard you, sir, but it is easier to get a whole tin
  than two sticks, sir. And they both cost the same price!
JOSIAH: (*Laughs quietly, realizing what Mugun Yaro means*) You are
  a smart kid, Mugun Yaro.
MUGUN YARO: You haven't seen anything, sir. I mean a real
  operation.
JOSIAH: Is Mugun Yaro your real name? You don't sound
  Hausa to me.
MUGUN YARO: Some Hausa friends of my master gave me the
  nickname. Master said that it was because I am very small
  and that nobody ever suspects anything when I borrow
  things from them. I am not Hausa. In fact, my village is
  only about ten miles from here.
JOSIAH: What is the meaning of Mugun?
MUGUN YARO: I don't know, but I like it. Are you going to stay
  with us for some time, sir? I mean, I will like it very much
  if you do.
JOSIAH: I don't know yet. Why will you like it if I stay on?
MUGUN YARO: Because my big master said that you are very
  powerful – that you have plenty of magical power with
  which you could 'borrow' a whole lorry-load of stuff!
JOSIAH: He told you that, did he?
MUGUN YARO: Please sir, don't tell him that I say anything
  about it, or I'll have much beating.
JOSIAH: No, I won't. How old are you, Mugun?
MUGUN YARO: Next Christmas will be my twelfth. I was born on
  Christmas Eve, so my mother said. That's why my real name
  is Abiodun.
JOSIAH: I see. Then you'll be eleven next Christmas.
MUGUN YARO. Yes, sir. Master said you used to operate in Lagos
  city?
JOSIAH: Yes.
MUGUN YARO: They say the sea there is so large that no-one

can see the end of it. And that the ships that travel on it to
Europe are larger and have more people than a whole city?

Baba Osa coming in humming

(*Whispers*) Master is coming. I must shut up, sir.

BABA OSA: Mugun Yaro!

MUGUN YARO: Yes sir!

BABA OSA: Mugun Yaro! Yaro!

MUGUN YARO: Great respect, sir!

BABA OSA: I have a dream!

MUGUN YARO: You wear a crown laced with jewels.

BABA OSA: I have a dream!

MUGUN YARO: You wear a regal robe!

BABA OSA: I have a dream!

MUGUN YARO: You walk with a staff of coral beads!

BABA OSA: And what?

MUGUN YARO: Your children shall bury you with great honour
and pomp!

BABA OSA: (*Bursts into laughter. Josiah and Mugun join in*) That's
right, Mugun. Now sing your song for Josiah.

MUGUN YARO: Mba mbamba kimba. Mba mbamba kimba.
Sakata ba doya ba. Kojere ba Mugun Yaro ba o.

JOSIAH: What are all these strange things you are saying?

BABA OSA: They are just passwords – mainly to train Mugun
Yaro's memory. Now we go down to work. (*Going off mic*)
The market must be nearly full now.

*fx: Door opens – the faraway noise of the market is heard. Bicycle bells
etc. pass occasionally*

BABA OSA: Josiah, we are going to do the three in one. (*Coming
on mic*) Mugun works, you chat; I observe. After the
operation, we split and meet at home. O.K.?

JOSIAH: O.K. What if anything goes wrong?

BABA OSA: I'll take care of that. You just pretend you've never
seen Mugun Yaro before. Mugun Yaro, keep your nerves,
I'll look after you. O.K.?

MUGUN YARO: All right, sir!

Fade out

Fade in

fx: General noise of the market place

MAMA TAIYE: (*Calls*) Good morning o, Mama Adisa.

MAMA ADISA: How do you do?

MAMA TAIYE: I'm all right. How is the family?

MAMA ADISA: Thank God. Everyone is well. I see Taiye comes with you. Is she on holidays already?

MAMA TAIYE: Yes – (*Whispers loudly*) Open your mouth and say hello. You schoolgirls are so dumb. You lack all the native manners and culture. God knows what they teach you in those schools of yours.

TAIYE: I just didn't want to interrupt your greetings – I might be accused of being forward or rude.

MAMA TAIYE: Never mind that. You always have an answer ready for everything. Are you going to say hello to Mama Adisa or stand there explaining things?

MAMA ADISA: Leave Taiye alone. The children of today are not like us. It requires a lot of patience to deal with them. Adisa is no different.

TAIYE: I wish you well, Mama Adisa.

MAMA ADISA: Thank you child – and all goes well with you?

TAIYE: Yes thank you, Ma.

fx: Peak market atmosphere and crowd – hold – fade under

MAMA TAIYE: (*In low voice*) Sh! Sh! Eh, Taiye, here he comes. Please, don't look.

TAIYE: Who?

MAMA TAIYE: The nameless one. The rat that feeds in full view of the householder. He has passed us now. I think he spots a victim nearby.

TAIYE: That small boy, ma?

MAMA TAIYE: Small boy! I've seen him steal a machine with heavy iron stand, while everyone but the owner was looking. His master is not around yet. Keep your eyes open.

TAIYE: The Jaguda Boys!

MAMA TAIYE: I say 'Shut up'! Look! I think that tall man is with the boy. He is a stranger. But he must be one too. (*Pause*) Aiee, they are both going for Mama Adisa. You'll see something you've never seen before today. Just watch. The rat has squatted behind her!

TAIYE: Mother, shall I go for the police then?

MAMA TAIYE: Sh! Sh!! Shut up!

TAIYE: But it's Mama Adisa!

MAMA TAIYE: Shut up! I say – we can do nothing!

fx: Peak effects – hold – fade under

JOSIAH: Have you Sasorabia perfume?

MAMA ADISA: Yes, by the dozen. I also have Titan, Jebo, Français, Jaman, all kinds of perfume in fact. And they are the cheapest in the whole market. Here, the Sasorabia – pure undiluted – smell (*Opens one for Josiah who scents it*).

JOSIAH: Unh unh . . . very very good. This is exactly what I want. How much for one?

MAMA ADISA: I sell them for twenty-five shillings each, but since it is you, well, my first-born is a boy; I leave it for you for twenty shillings.

JOSIAH: Fifteen shillings.

MAMA ADISA: Please don't be like that. You men never know how to price things. You cut five shillings off just like that, eh! . . well, take it, as a special concession for you, because you are my first customer this morning. I'll wrap it for you. (*Makes a move to wrap it*)

JOSIAH: Not yet! I can only pay thirteen shillings.

MAMA ADISA: What's this? I didn't get them from smugglers, you know. Don't you want me to eat something myself?

JOSIAH: I want everybody to eat a little.

MAMA ADISA: Put a shilling more and take it at fourteen shillings. And that's selling at cost price.

JOSIAH: I really can't put a shilling more.

MAMA ADISA: Eh, listen, handsome young man! I can guess what you want for it. You want to prepare love charm with it, so you can charm any woman, all women you desire. O yes! Yes!! Don't I know . . . well, I tell you, it is more potent than anything I know. But, in buying the ingredients for love charm, one must not be too tight-fisted. In the long run women can't stand tight-fisted men, you know. (*Gives a phoney laugh*) Well, I bless you my man, God bless you and whatsoever you are using it for. Take it for thirteen shillings, but don't spread the news.

JOSIAH: Thank you. But I want more than one. I am a petty trader from a far away village myself.

MAMA ADISA: Don't give me that. You look every inch a dashing young man from some city . . . Lagos, I might say.

JOSIAH: Eh! (*Laughs*) Not all villagers carry the emblem.

MAMA ADISA: Of course not. I'm only joking. Well pick as many as you want and I'll make the addition.

JOSIAH: I'll want two dozen. But it will have to be at the rate of ten shillings each. I will pay now if that's agreed.

MAMA ADISA: I can't catch that very well. Do you come here to buy perfume, or are you just wandering about the market? Ten shillings, he says! You realize that you are the first one to deal with me today? And that this is going to set the pattern of sales for me for the whole day? Please don't spoil my day. May the spirit of wealth abide with you . . . Take it at twelve shillings, and I will be able to sell only a dozen to you, because it is at a loss.

JOSIAH: No, I can't. You don't want to do a business with me. I must go. I have other things to buy.

MAMA ADISA: Go? Go where? You call yourself a trader, and you behave like the first-born of poverty itself. Early in the morning! You wretch, with neck like that of a giraffe; and knees knocking at opposite angles . . . You never intended to buy anything in the first place . . . you bastard; eyes like an owl's and back view like that of a camel. Profits and prosperity shall never come your way! (*Pause – to herself*) Oh my Creator, what have I done to deserve this! I performed all the rites before leaving home. I hope this trend of evil influence will not continue today. God, my conscience is clear as the spring water. (*Pause*) I better sort out the loose change ready. It is always dangerous to open one's money bag in front of customers. (*Feels her waist; pause*) Where is it? . . . my money-bag! Oh, am I dreaming or what? Oh it's been cut! (*Shouts*) Oh! people of the market come o, I'm bedevilled! I'm finished! I'm lost! My money bag is gone! Help me, anybody! (*Bursts into wailing tears*) Hurricane strikes at my homestead. Police! Police!

fx: *General rumpus in the market – peak market noise – hold – fade under*

TAIYE: Mother! See what's happened to Mama Adisa! We could have prevented it.

MAMA TAIYE: Shut up, I say. It is not our business. One doesn't protect other's heads while the eagle snatches one's own away.

TAIYE: Mother, but it could happen to you too.

MAMA TAIYE: It will happen to me, if you keep on. Well, I tell

you something. I live here; and those Jagudas can sort me
out. They are most dangerous and mean, when seeking
revenge against anyone who interferes with their business.
The former bicycle repairer from Arigbajo tried to tackle
them. One by one his bicycles disappeared. They then raided
his home, taking everything, even the brooms. He too has
since disappeared, leaving his young wife and child in the
care of his relatives. Is that what you want for me, Taiye?

TAIYE: But they needn't know who reports them to the police.

MAMA TAIYE: They'll find out sooner or later. Besides, I'm sure,
the tall one, who pretends to bargain, knew that we saw the
small boy who squatted behind Mama Adisa. Oh, they are
as clever as they are evil.

TAIYE: Now I understand, but it was Mama Adisa.

MAMA TAIYE: No buts – she'd have done the same as me! And
talk about something else or shut up.

TAIYE: All right, Ma!

Fade out

Fade in Baba Osa, humming a local tune carelessly to himself

MUGUN YARO: (*Breathlessly runs in on mic calling*) Master! I did it,
master. I did it. Here's the money bag.

fx: Sound of money bag passed over

BABA OSA: Relax, and stop beaming like an idiot. I saw
everything. I watched it all happen just as I planned it. But
you nearly goofed it, you clumsy son of a goat. (*In an
unfriendly tone*) Come here! Give me your left ear.

MUGUN YARO: Please, master, what have I done wrong? I did
everything as I was told throughout the operation.

Baba Osa takes Mugun's ear. Mugun groans in pain

MUGUN YARO: My ear! Ooh . . . it hurts . . .

BABA OSA: How many times have I told you never to dip your
whole hand in people's pockets? Did I not tell you always to
use fingers and fingers only?

MUGUN YARO: (*Groaning as Baba Osa squeezes harder*) Yes, you did, sir.

BABA OSA: Then why did you disobey me? I saw your whole
arm buried in the woman's skirt, or *didn't* I? (*Squeezes harder*)

MUGUN YARO: (*In pain*) Yes, master. The skirt was a long one and I had to lift her outer wrapper to get at it. I'm sorry, master.

BABA OSA: (*Throws Mugun free*) You very nearly bungled the whole thing – a perfect set-up like that with nothing for you to worry about . . . Now where is Josiah? He ought to have been here by now.

MUGUN YARO: I left him still bargaining with the woman.

BABA OSA: I saw him leave just before the woman began her Jeremiah wailing. I hope he is all right . . . (*Pause*) I think that's him coming.

JOSIAH: Ah, Baba Osa! (*Roaring with laughter, coming in on mic*) This is one of the smoothest operations I have ever been involved in for a long time.

BABA OSA: Never mind that. I planned it and I know. But why are you so late in coming?

JOSIAH: I took a long detour and got the way mixed up. I know everything was all right. (*Loudly and boastfully*) No animal ever waylays the tiger.

BABA OSA: Josi! Josi!! Josi the torrent that clears all in its path!

JOSIAH: My homage to you, Baba Osa. Sea never dries. Butterfly will never fall over. (*Both laugh heartily*) Eh, I'm beginning to feel hungry now!

BABA OSA: First things first. We must count the money now. Mugun Yaro, lock the door and bring the key. Not that anyone dares show up here uninvited, but one mustn't tempt them. (*They laugh*)

: Sound of door being locked, then of coins being poured on the floor

JOSIAH: Oh, there are notes in it as well.

BABA OSA: Some of the papers are not money. (*Counts out loud*) Seventeen pounds in notes. Now the coins. (*Begins to count without using words, only the sound*) Give me a hand, Josiah.

: Clinks of coins

JOSIAH: With money, I don't mind at all. Hey, but I'm starving now.

BABA OSA: My girl will bring food in a minute.

JOSIAH: I never like to eat food prepared by whores. I don't trust them.

BABA OSA: She is not a whore. She is a respectably married woman. You'll like her. Look at Mugun Yaro's eyes coming

out of their sockets at the sight of money! Mugun Yaro, go
prepare the goat in the yard ready for barbecue.

MUGUN YARO: (*Cheerfully going off mic*) Yes, master.

JOSIAH: Oh, I have missed the counting.

BABA OSA: You can leave the rest, I'll count it. I can sing and
count at the same time. (*He counts the coins*) There you are.
Five pounds eight shillings in coins, that makes twenty-two
pounds eight shillings altogether. Not bad, eh?

JOSIAH: I'd never have guessed that that poorly dressed woman
was so loaded.

BABA OSA: I can smell them out no matter what their clothes . . .
It is a matter of instinct based on experience in this part.
(*Pause*) Mugun Yaro!

MUGUN YARO: (*Running in on mic*) Yes, master! I come, sir.

BABA OSA: How are you getting on with your cousin?

MUGUN YARO: (*With enthusiasm*) It's already on the fire, sir.
(*Baba Osa and Josiah laugh*)

BABA OSA: Good, good! Go tell Awanatu that I want some food
now – also that I have a guest.

MUGUN YARO: (*Going off mic*) Yes, sir.

BABA OSA: Take the short cut across the yard.

MUGUN YARO: (*Off mic*) Yes, sir.

JOSIAH: But this boy appears clever.

BABA OSA: That's the result of tough training. He was as dull
and slow-witted as a lamb when he first came here.

JOSIAH: I still can't stop marvelling at the steadiness of his
nerves, when he was doing the operation on that woman.

BABA OSA: Oh yes, he pulled it off all right. But even though I
have warned him always to use fingers and fingers only, he
stuck his mosquito-like arm into the woman's pocket. The
woman did feel something I'm sure, but was just too absorbed
with your talking. Your contribution at that point was
crucial.

JOSIAH: But the so-called famous 'fingers alone' theory can be a
serious limitation and sometimes impractical?

BABA OSA: I don't think so, and neither did the old timers. The
good old Jaguda himself, may he rest in peace, was the first
exponent of 'fingers'. Akin Devil, Sanni Wallet, Jo Big-
Spender, Obeche slow-motion-lightning and several other top
men of our profession are all finger-men. Tell me *one* who is
not!

JOSIAH: Baba Osa, nearly all the boys you've just mentioned talk in praise of 'fingers'; but they perform according to the situation. For instance, I've seen Akin Devil give a virtuoso performance at Oyingbo market in full view of everyone. Believe it or not, he disappeared right inside the huge garment of a Hausa cattle merchant to cut the poor man's bulging wallet. For a good three minutes, there stood the merchant on what looked like four legs – chewing his kola-nut with ease, Akin did it – in his own way. Yet, as you said, he always shouts 'fingers only'.

BABA OSA: Yes – okay, you can always experiment and improvise, after you've become experienced; but the young ones, I maintain, should be reared on the 'fingers' system. It makes for discipline, and I want discipline for my boy.

JOSIAH: Yes, you are right there, Baba Osa. But I would go easy with that boy, he is good. Eh, I am hungry.

BABA OSA: So am I too – but while we are waiting let's have a bit of palm wine, Josi.

OSIAH: On empty stomachs?

BABA OSA: Try it and see. This is no ordinary palm wine. It is straight from the tree undiluted, a great appetizer.

x: Pouring wine into a calabash

OSIAH: O.K.

BABA OSA: Well . . . libation first. This is to Earth, to the witches and the wizards of the market! (*He drops some palm wine*) To mother earth, who swallowed up the bones of our colleagues, who joined the white man's army and never came back. Let them rest in peace, wherever they lie. Be it India, Abyssinia, Burma or the high seas. (*Drops some palm wine*)

OSIAH: Amin, amin.

BABA OSA: Lastly, to you and me – our friendship, Josi (*Drinks*) Here, Josi.

OSIAH: Amin, amin. (*Drinks*)

BABA OSA: Josi. You know, since you arrived, we haven't really talked yet. Now what exactly brought you here?

OSIAH: That's a big question. The story is long and complicated. But I'll spare you the details. The only thing that matters is that I'm giving up the profession.

BABA OSA: (*Laughs*) You!

OSIAH: Me, Baba Osa. Fifteen years and I haven't much to

show for it. No regrets, of course, but I've been thinking a
lot. I came here because last time I was in prison my mind
always went to you – out of all the boys I knew. But for you,
I would have joined the army like most of the boys of the
profession.

BABA OSA: Well, I'm glad I stopped you. This war is not for us.
I come from a long line of warriors – the real professionals –
as you know. No cowardice in my veins – only prudence. But
what difference will it make to us who wins this time?
Hitler, English, American or any other son of a bitch you
care to name. It's the white man's war. Let them fight it out
– and we can take on whichever master comes along. Josiah,
you know, now I am yearning for a change of Governor, be
he German, or a Spaniard like in Fernando. (*Both laugh
hysterically*)

JOSIAH: Baba Osa, you will never change. (*Both laugh*) Jeri!

BABA OSA: Jeri coco.

JOSIAH: Who no know.

BABA OSA: He go know.

JOSIAH: Abumbu yanya.

BABA OSA: Water of alekiriti.

JOSIAH: He go make them sick, he go make us cure. (*Laughs*)
But seriously, Baba Osa, I'm quitting the profession.

BABA OSA: Yes, we all give it a thought now and again. But
what else does one do? Any idea?

JOSIAH: I really don't know, but Allah will make a way for his
own somehow.

BABA OSA: But that is not a good . . .

*fx: Four very odd light knocks. Pause. Then a short tune is whistled from
outside*

BABA OSA: Oh, it's only Mugun.

fx: Door unlocks and opens

Why did you knock like that?

AWANATU: (*Coming in on mic*) He didn't. I did. I didn't mean to
frighten you.

BABA OSA: Who's frightened? Come on in and meet my friend
from Lagos. Josiah, this is Awanatu, my own.

JOSIAH: Hello, dear one.

AWANATU: Hello sir, my knees on the floor for you, sir.

JOSIAH: Please rise. You do well; you have been looking after my friend. I wondered how he began to get pot-bellied, now I know it's good feeding.

AWANATU: (*Proudly, giggling and girlishly*) I do try my best. When I can get hold of him, sir! (*All laugh*)

BABA OSA: (*Going off mic*) Josiah, you and Mugun can carry on with the meal. Eat. Mugun, get the food. I've got something important to discuss with Awanatu . . . in here, Awanatu . . .

AWANATU: (*Still on mic*) What is it? Can't it wait?

BABA OSA: No, it's pressing. I need you in the bedroom, Awanatu.

AWANATU: But Mugun said you were hungry; that's why I rushed things . . . your favourite. Asoro with palaver sauce of kano fish and shrimps!

BABA OSA: Hum . . . that is something . . . but come first . . . this is important.

Fade as all laugh as Awanatu goes off mic

: Fade in − Josiah and Mugun Yaro eating and drinking − sound of plates etc.

JOSIAH: This is a very delicious sauce. Baba Osa doesn't know what he's missing! Bush women are famous cooks.

MUGUN YARO: Sh! Sh! She is not a bush woman, sir. Master says she was born in the Gold Coast. They sometimes call her Sisi Accra.

JOSIAH: But she lives here in the bush.

MUGUN YARO: Yes, sir. (*Pause: eating goes on*) You said you will take me to Lagos, sir.

JOSIAH: Did I? Pass your barbecue. (*Cuts a piece and bites it*) Hum . . . it is quite delicious. Now, why do you want to go to Lagos?

MUGUN YARO: To get more civilized; and besides, I don't like it here. It is only the master that is making me happy here. Kids here won't play games with me, I have no friends like I had back in my village. I have to be on my own all the time. But don't tell my master, because he doesn't like me to mix with other kids in the neighbourhood. He said they will lead me astray.

JOSIAH: (*Chuckles*) Tell me, do you want to remain a Jaguda boy all your life?

MUGUN YARO: I don't know, sir. Perhaps I'll like to become a
     real robber, but I'm afraid of getting shot like Bramah Daji.
JOSIAH: Oh him, yes. So you really want to go to Lagos?
MUGUN YARO: Yes, sir.
JOSIAH: I can take you to Lagos, but you won't be allowed to
     pick pockets.
MUGUN YARO: What shall I do then?
JOSIAH: Well, I can hire you to some big Saro man as a house-
     boy, and he will send you to school in return for your
     services. How is that?
MUGUN YARO: School, sir?
JOSIAH: Yes, school.
MUGUN YARO: That will be very nice. But I can still pick
     pockets after school hours, sir. Can't I?
JOSIAH: No. You can't.
MUGUN YARO: Why, sir?
JOSIAH: Because . . . er . . . you see . . . any kid caught thieving
     in Lagos is thrown into the Lagoon with a heavy stone
     round his neck.
MUGUN YARO: Oh!
JOSIAH: Yes, that is the Lagos Law.

*fx: Three heavy aggressive bangs on the door. Pause, four more bangs in
     quick succession − pause − inside door opens*

BABA OSA: (*Coming in on mic*) That must be the Police. Awanatu,
     you stay there: and if they flush you out, say nothing,
     remember that.
AWANATU: Yes!
BABA OSA: Just stay where you are and don't panic.

fx: Door bangs again

LAYI: (*Off mic*) Open, open the door in the name of Alake and
     his Council, open up.
BABA OSA: (*Going off mic*) All right, all right, we are opening for
     you.

fx: Door unlocked and opened

     Corporal Layi, it is you. (*Coming in on mic*) Please come right
     in. What's all the banging about?
LAYI: Don't move anybody, this is a raid.

BABA OSA: (*Bursts into loud laughter*) Corporal Layi. A raid? What raid? Please relax. What's the matter?

LAYI: You know what is the matter. You are coming to the station with me, now.

BABA OSA: Me? Come now, Corporal Layi, show me a bit of respect. Anyway, I don't suppose you are serious.

LAYI: I am this time.

BABA OSA: O yeah?

LAYI: (*Agitated*) Where were you this morning?

BABA OSA: Now tell me what this is all about, and we can discuss it like two gentlemen.

LAYI: I'm taking you in for stealing in the market this morning. I don't want to use the handcuffs, but I will if I have to!

fx: Jingle of handcuffs

BABA OSA: Now, don't overdo things. Go back to the Station. Tell Sergeant Bello I'll come to see him later.

LAYI: I'm in charge of this case. You are not seeing anyone later.

BABA OSA: Quit being childish, Corporal Layi. I'm being civil with you and you are still carrying on. What have you got on me?

LAYI: This time I have plenty on you. There are reliable eye witnesses waiting to testify against you and your little rat!

UGUN YARO: (*Startled*) Who? Me, sir?

LAYI: Yes, you little rat of the market.

UGUN YARO: I have never left this house today, sir.

BABA OSA: Leave the kid out of it and get out of here before I throw you out!

LAYI: You dare not touch the King's uniform.

OSIAH: Hey! You sound like two real old pals. Why don't you cool tempers and talk talkie eh? Baba Osa, you know the law is the law and constables have jobs to do.

BABA OSA: O.K. Josi. I think you've got a point there. Now Corporal Layi, I guess I have to see *you*, now, and Sergeant Bello later.

LAYI: Just as you choose.

BABA OSA: Come closer . . . (*Begins to speak in a low voice*) There wasn't much in the loot you know –

LAYI: If you want to make a deal make a deal. What's the secrecy? Speak to me loud and clear.

BABA OSA: All right! (*In a loud voice*) There wasn't much in the

bag – a few pound notes and several coins – eleven pounds
in all. O.K.?

LAYI: (*In a normal voice*) The Lagos woman swore it was twenty-
four pounds and some of her important papers. So, give me
another.

BABA OSA: O.K. What's your offer?

LAYI: You are making the offer.

BABA OSA: You know, I still have to see your boss . . .

LAYI: That's no concern of mine.

BABA OSA: Eh! What's the matter with you today, Corporal –
showing off in front of my friend, or what? (*Pause*) (*Going off
mic*) O.K., wait here.

fx: Internal door opens – noise of chest opened and closed – door closes

BABA OSA: (*Coming in on mic*) Well, here it is. We are all men of
the market – no cheating, nothing underhand, everything on
the level. This is your big pay day Corporal Layi. Here – for
you alone, three pounds.

*fx: Rustle of pound notes – suddenly, Corporal Layi blows his whistle
with all his vigour. It is a sign for Sergeant Momo, who had come
with Corporal Layi, but was waiting outside unknown to Baba Osa –
ready to pounce on hearing signal*
*Noise of policemen bursting in, pushing the door in, with violent
crashes all over the place*

SGT. MOMO: (*Rushing in on mic*) Stay still, everybody.

fx: Corporal Layi wrestling with Baba Osa

CORPORAL LAYI: (*Out of breath struggling with Baba Osa*) He trie
to bribe me, Sergeant!

MUGUN YARO: (*Starts crying*) They want to kill my master! Oh
God, they want to kill him.

JOSIAH: You know, you have no right to do this to him! You
know you have no right, Sergeant?

SGT. MOMO: You wait your turn, lawyer.

fx: Amidst the struggle comes the clicking of handcuffs

LAYI: I've got him handcuffed!

BABA OSA: (*Breathing heavily*) Oh God, you disgrace me like this
in my own house.

SGT. MOMO: Stand up. You asked for it. Now, where is the rest
the loot?

LAYI: I think in that room somewhere, sergeant.

BABA OSA: Don't enter my room, you have no warrant, you hear that? I'll give it to you. Just don't enter my room.

SGT. MOMO: That's better. Where is it then?

BABA OSA: (*Breathing heavily*) Mugun, open the box in the room and bring me the money bag in here.

MUGUN YARO: (*Going off mic*) Yes, sir!

fx: Internal door opens – noise of chest opened and closed – door closes

SGT. MOMO: You should have done that in the first place.

MUGUN YARO: (*Coming on mic*) Here, master.

BABA OSA: Give it to Sergeant . . . eh . . . sorry . . . Sergeant . . .

SGT. MOMO: (*Indignant*) Sergeant R. W. Momo, the sweeper, the cop you *cannot* see '*later*'. Remember that. (*Grabs the money bag from Mugun*)

SGT. MOMO: Anything else, Corporal Layi?

LAYI: That's all, Sergeant. We've got the 'Big Fish' hooked, Sarge.

SGT. MOMO: Well done . . . (*Pause*) Let's go.

BABA OSA: Sgt. Momo, (*Pleadingly*) please, can I have a word with my friend about my belongings and other little matters.

SGT. MOMO: (*Hesitates*) All right, make it snappy and stay in view.

BABA OSA: (*Close to Josiah and whispering*) Leave my keys with Awanatu. Disappear with Mugun Yaro for a fortnight at least. There is no problem for me. See what I mean?

JOSIAH: Yes, I do . . . no problem.

LAYI: They are saying something, Sarge.

SGT. MOMO: O.K. That's enough chattering there, you two.

LAYI: Come on or I'll have to drag you out of here.

BABA OSA: (*Deliberately*) Corporal Layi.

LAYI: Yes.

BABA OSA: You'll never be a Sergeant . . . 'cause you have no initiative.

Chuckle from Josiah

LAYI: Oh God! You hear that, Sarge! He is putting a curse on me, Sarge. He put his little finger in his mouth before he said it, Sarge.

SGT. MOMO: Don't worry about it: he is not on the Police Promotion Board, is he? (*Going off mic*) Off we go.

LAYI & MOMO: (*Going off mic pushing Baba Osa*) C'mon, you.
BABA OSA: (*Struggling, as they go off mic*) Don't push me!
JOSIAH: Good luck, Brother!

fx: Door slams

MUGUN YARO: (*In tears*) They are going to lock my master up.
JOSIAH: Keep quiet and start packing your things.
AWANATU: (*Approaching mic from the bedroom in a very agitated state*)
    They have taken him away. I heard everything. What are
    we going to do?
JOSIAH: You just do as I say. We'll lock up the place. Baba Osa
    will come to you for the keys later.
AWANATU: (*Suspicious*) When is later?
JOSIAH: Never mind . . .
AWANATU: Where are you going?
JOSIAH: Never mind . . .
AWANATU: (*Infuriated*) Never mind! . . . Never mind! Your
    friend got arrested right in front of you, and all you can
    think of is running away – and taking his boy.
JOSIAH: Baba Osa will explain everything to you later.
AWANATU: Yes indeed, when he is rotting in prison! Mugun
    Yaro, will you desert your master? Or will you stay here and
    let me look after you?
MUGUN YARO: (*Confused and in tears*) I . . . I . . .
JOSIAH: Oh woman! We have no time. But listen. Mugun Yaro
    and I pulled the job this morning. And the police naturally
    assumed that I was Baba Osa. They have taken so much for
    granted, because they had been gunning for Baba Osa. They
    will be here the minute they realize their mistake – any time
    now. That's why Baba Osa asked me to disappear and take
    Mugun with me. Don't you see, Baba Osa is innocent this
    time – so they'll have to release him! (*Laughs*)

fx: Crockery being collected

AWANATU: (*Laughing moving round mic*) Baba Osa always beats th
    police – he'll come for me!
JOSIAH: Now, Awanatu, you'll have to lock up right now becaus
    we have no time.
AWANATU: All right. I'll come back later for these.
JOSIAH: O.K. Ready, Mugun?

MUGUN YARO: Ready, sir.
JOSIAH: Right. Let's all get out of here.

fx: Door opened and slammed shut and locked

JOSIAH: Remember, Awanatu, you have seen nothing, you have
   heard nothing. Baba Osa will come. Goodbye for now.
AWANATU: Goodbye Mugun Yaro. Josiah, goodbye.
MUGUN YARO: Goodbye.
JOSIAH: Goodbye. Hey! If we catch the train tonight, Mugun,
   you'll have supper in Lagos.
MUGUN YARO: Lagos?
JOSIAH: Yes, Lagos. C'mon.

Beyond the Line

LABAN ERAPU

Laban Erapu, *born in 1944, was educated in Uganda and took a degree in English at Makerere before going to Edinburgh University to work on Afro-Caribbean Literature. He is now teaching literature at Makerere, where he is also a member of the* Travelling Theatre. *He has had one novel published,* Restless Feet *(Oxford University Press) and some poetry in* Poems from East Africa *(Heinemann).*

Recorded Sunday 20th June 1971

CAST

Dr Baasa – Cosmo Pieterse
Mrs Baasa – Musindo Mwinyipembe
Jenny Baasa – Taiwo Ajai
Mike – Abdi Abubakar
Brenda – Rane Dube
Silva – Renu Setna

SOUND EFFECTS
Door
Trolley
Crockery

Place: The Baasas' Home in East Africa
Time: The present, one afternoon

fx: Door closes

DR. BAASA: (*Coming in on mic*) You don't smoke, I know. Mind if I do?

BRENDA: Oh no, Dr Baasa, of course not.

DR. BAASA: Thank you, sit down.

BRENDA: Thank you.

DR. BAASA: Smoking is one of my few remaining vices.

BRENDA: It's not right for a doctor like you to smoke.

DR. BAASA: More politician than doctor now, I would say.

BRENDA: I wish more people would give it up.

DR. BAASA: That's what I like about Asian girls: you are so correct, so well brought up.

BRENDA: Is that a compliment?

DR. BAASA: Sure, of the highest order. You don't smoke, you don't drink, you don't go about with boys – what more could any parent want?

BRENDA: But your daughter Jenny doesn't drink or smoke.

DR. BAASA: I wouldn't swear to that – not after having seen her string around a series of boy friends. Mark you, I don't think it is an entirely bad thing for a girl her age – having hundreds of boys, I mean. It will teach her one or two things about life.

BRENDA: I bet you wouldn't say so if your wife had been like that as a girl.

DR. BAASA: But she was! She was just like Jenny when I first met her. I was a medical student then, back in the early fifties. She was a student nurse, still in her first year, but already everyone in the hospital knew her for her friendliness. In Medical School we had a special name for her: we called her the Queen of Hearts. But pardon me, they said you had something to tell me and here am I clucking away like an old hen.

BRENDA: It's all right, go on. I would love to hear all about your romance.

DR. BAASA: No, Brenda, it's you young ones who should be talking about romance. We're old, we should do the listening.

BRENDA: Old, Dr Bassa? You're not old! Why, you're just in your prime of life!

DR. BAASA: Thank you, that's most flattering but not really true.
Oh, you should have seen me in those days. I wasn't like all
these serious minded young men who are so damn anxious
to become doctors and lawyers and all the rest of it. I was in
the GGG!

BRENDA: The GGG?

DR. BAASA: Go-Get-Gang, isn't there such a thing anymore?

BRENDA: Go-Get-Gang!

DR. BAASA: Your father would have told you if he hadn't been
one of those we called 'scholar-boys'. *We* only looked inside
a book to pass exams. From Medical School we would head
straight to where we could have fun and trouble. Cinemas we
regarded as too tame, too conventional. So we went for the
night clubs, the bars, the Nurses' Hostel and the Y.W.C.A.
If any one was interested in a girl, we invaded her home like
an army of occupation. It got so bad that many parents
hated us on sight and locked up their daughters, and the
only girls we could go about with were rebels like us.

BRENDA: I believe you are making up all this to shock me.

DR. BAASA: How disappointing, I thought you would say what a
great guy I must have been.

BRENDA: I thought you were going to tell me about courting
your wife.

DR. BAASA: Ah, that was a quiet affair. The day I went to see
Mary's parents, I was as discreet as a mouse. The GGG knew
nothing about my plans, for I didn't want a battalion to
escort me, though I felt I could have done with some moral
support. You know, Mary's father was high in the circle of
the saved ones. You can imagine how nice and polite I was,
all in a cold sweat. But Mary was very good to me. She
introduced me as the son of Yona Baasa – well known among
the saved ones – and said I was going to be a doctor the year
after.

BRENDA: You mean you 'declared your intentions' there and
then?

DR. BAASA: Oh no, that would have been a sure way to lose her.
My father did that some weeks after – at the Church
Convention, I believe.

BRENDA: And when did you propose to Mary?

DR. BAASA: Would you believe it – on the tennis court, the first
time we met.

BRENDA: You were fast!

DR. BAASA: You know what – that year *I* won the tournament, and a bride.

BRENDA: You married before graduating?

DR. BAASA: There's nothing like marriage when it comes to graduation.

BRENDA: But it's difficult when you're so young, isn't it?

DR. BAASA: It's very difficult, so why wait for wrinkles and grey hair to make it worse? You should try it and see. A lovely girl like you should get lots of young men breaking their legs to reach the altar first.

BRENDA: How did you manage?

DR. BAASA: Oh, it was a little trying when Mike was born. I was doing my internship and Mary was just going into her last year. He couldn't have chosen a worse time, I suppose, but then Mike has always been considerate. It's Jenny who brought all the headaches with her: she nearly got born on the plane to London, she fought like a boy at school, she always just scraped through her exams and now it's her string of boy friends that is the main worry. God knows if she will get through to graduation. But I'm not supposed to be doing the talking – you are – so what's it all about?

BRENDA: Well, you see – you know, Jenny and I have been friends for many years now. I think she's very intelligent and sensitive.

DR. BAASA: Come, come, be a brave girl and stop beating about the bush. Jenny's virtues are doubtful at the best of times anyway! Don't be shy. You and your brother have been in and out of our home for many years now. And Mike and Jenny tell us a great deal about your life together in the university.

BRENDA: Yes, we're very good friends.

DR. BAASA: I know Brenda, I'm not too old to tell young love when I see it.

BRENDA: I don't know what you're driving at.

DR. BAASA: Oh? I beg your pardon.

BRENDA: Dr Baasa, we've got a problem.

DR. BAASA: Problem?

BRENDA: We need your help – I mean, parental advice.

DR. BAASA: Let's hear it from the beginning, shall we?

BRENDA: Dr Baasa, what do you feel about mixed marriage?

DR. BAASA: You mean interracial marriage.

BRENDA: Isn't it the same thing?

DR. BAASA: Not to my mind. One is distinctly non-political, unnecessarily evasive and most unfortunately implies confusion and a mix-up of values. The other faces the issue squarely and is both political and diplomatic – which is what racial relations are about.

BRENDA: You mean they are political and diplomatic but not personal?

DR. BAASA: I was only stating my preference in terminology.

BRENDA: Well, what do you feel about interracial marriage, if that is what you prefer to call it?

DR. BAASA: I don't know what I *feel* about it, but I can tell you what I *think*. In principle, I don't object to anything that will bring different races closer. And nothing could be closer than coming together to breed a new race.

BRENDA: You make it sound unpleasant.

DR. BAASA: Not at all – we all marry to breed, that's a fact. But marriage is by no means the easiest way to bring the races closer. Come to think of it, the breeding of an intermediate race could actually lead to the pushing further apart of the parent races – especially when it comes to us black people.

BRENDA: In countries like Britain and America you and I would both be grouped as coloureds.

DR. BAASA: I know, and that indiscriminate lumping together has tended to divide us amongst ourselves.

BRENDA: That's not true.

DR. BAASA: Perhaps not on an international and ideological level, but it has on the personal.

BRENDA: I think you're being too pessimistic. It can't all be politics. Surely there's still such a thing as love?

DR. BAASA: Love is all right until the honeymoon is over and real marriage starts. When you are of different races, people never recognize that your marriage is a private and personal thing. You each have to be defensive about your race, and courteous about your partners. Then you're expected to be exceptions and always in tip-top form. And there's the very great problem of children. It is your responsibility to realize from the very beginning what problems they'll be faced with as they grow up. In your eyes they will be attractive beyond comparison, but they will also be called names – half-caste or coloured, that's nasty for the child. And it will pain you as much as them. It will pain you even more when you see how perplexed they are standing on the edge of two worlds, neither of which makes them feel they belong. Love doesn't alter any of that!

BRENDA: So you wouldn't approve.

DR. BAASA: I would advise against it.

BRENDA: Would you use your power to stop it?

DR. BAASA: If marriage is private and personal, I can't see how I could possibly have the power to stop anyone from marrying whom he chooses.

BRENDA: Not even your children?

DR. BAASA: Not even my children – in principle, that is.

BRENDA: Oh, and in practice?

DR. BAASA: How should I know? It hasn't happened.

BRENDA: But supposing it did.

DR. BAASA: Well, it hasn't, has it? You still haven't told me what this is all about, or have you forgotten that we came in here at your specific request?

BRENDA: I think I now know what I wanted to find out.

DR. BAASA: And am I going to find out what you wanted to know?

BRENDA: Dr Baasa, what would you say if I told you that one of your children was considering getting married?

DR. BAASA: Beyond the line?

BRENDA: Yes, beyond the line.

DR. BAASA: Which one?

BRENDA: I thought you meant the racial line.

DR. BAASA: I mean, is it Mike or Jenny you're referring to?

BRENDA: It doesn't matter which, it was just a question.

DR. BAASA: Then I have no straight answer to offer.

BRENDA: Ooh!

DR. BAASA: But I will tell you this: if it were not for obvious reasons, there's no other girl I would sooner have for a daughter-in-law.

BRENDA: Is that a compliment?

DR. BAASA: What else?

BRENDA: Thanks a lot, but I'm out of the running. And by 'obvious reasons' I suppose you mean the colour of my skin? What has happened to all the races in this country getting together to build a new nation? Was it just politics, just talk, talk, talk?

DR. BAASA: Steady, Brenda, don't get over-excited. Let me offer you some parental advice. You're young, Brenda, young and full of promise. The best in life is yet ahead of you. It's up to you to be on the lookout and reach for it when it comes your way. You are a Goan, you are almost white and you are flying high. Don't look down now and get mixed up with us black people of the earth. Fly to some land of snow – Canada, America, anywhere where the wind won't blow dust into your eyes.

BRENDA: I didn't know you were capable of such sarcasm.

DR. BAASA: Don't you know: what *you* can do *we* can do as well, as the Women's Lib would say. But to be perfectly serious, marriage is no laughing matter. It's all right standing on the platform and talking about getting together to build a new nation and all the rest of it. But it never helps to mix business with pleasure – politics and marriage can be very uneasy bedmates. Tell me, you and Mike are not in some kind of trouble, are you?

BRENDA: *Me* and Mike – what do you mean? Dr Baasa, I would like you to understand that Mike and I are only good friends. There's nothing at all between us. What sort of girl do you think I am?

DR. BAASA: So it's Jenny, then. (*Laughing*) I wonder who it is this time.

BRENDA: I think she's grown to be very fond of my brother Silva.

DR. BAASA: What, that –

BRENDA: That what? There's nothing the matter with Silva. He's a little shy, that's all. Jenny herself told me.

DR. BAASA: Don't make me laugh – who ever believes what Jenny says?

BRENDA: Dr Baasa, I have reasons to believe they are serious about it.

DR. BAASA: Ooh. And are they really planning to get married?

BRENDA: Don't you think they could make a wonderful couple?

DR. BAASA: I believe they could make a wonderful muddle. You and your feminine sentiments! What do you think you know about marriage, let alone mixed marriage?

BRENDA: I thought you preferred to call it interracial marriage?

DR. BAASA: Yes, *if* it *was* a marriage – this would be a classic mix-up in a Fools' Paradise.

BRENDA: You're not being fair to them. Surely you know that where there's love there's a way.

DR. BAASA: Spare me the clichés, please. I don't even know what you mean by love anymore.

BRENDA: *You* don't have to know it for *them*.

DR. BAASA: I was referring to your generation as a whole. Of course we too once held such silly romantic notions, picked up from cheap paperbacks and glossy magazines and the silver screen and all the rest of them. But you young people of today have gone overboard with 'doing your own thing' as you put it. All that you're capable of is addiction to strange habits. You have made Love a public thing and a password to self-dissipation. You've been deafened by the din of jukeboxes bellowing rock music and blinded by the ultraviolet lights in the discotheques. You see white as whiter than white, and you think you can deceive the world with corny phrases like *Black is Beautiful* and *Make Love not War*. Dazed with drugs and drink and lust, you have lost the capacity for enjoyment. You have lost the value of love.

BRENDA: You speak of love as though it were a commodity your generation stowed away in Swiss banks with your ill-gotten wages of Independence.

DR. BAASA: You are very brave to say such a thing to a Cabinet Minister.

BRENDA: What has a poor girl like me to be afraid of? Besides, I believe you're speaking to me as a father and not as Minister of Health. Of course you might think I'm a bit of a mental case requiring medical care. But how can you think that of me? Just because I happen to believe that people should be free to marry who they want, regardless of colour or creed? If only more people would stop simplifying racial relations by putting up all these black-and-white stereotyped defences.

DR. BAASA: (*Clapping*) Bravo! But you would do the same.

BRENDA: Me? I am a liberal!

DR. BAASA: Liberal! Shall I tell you what I think of you liberals? I think you are bloody hypocrites. Because you're in love with your little selves, you imagine you're in love with the whole world. Because you're short-sighted and blind, you imagine you've looked beyond the colour of man's skin and perceived a beauty too deep for other eyes to see. You've made us the helpless recipients of your liberalism, just as you made us the bearers of your prejudices. You bloody hypocrites, who are you to presume you're doing us a favour?

BRENDA: I would rather be a 'bloody' hypocrite than a blasted racist.

DR. BAASA: I'm not a racist.

BRENDA: Yes, you are! Why can't I be black like you if I want to?

DR. BAASA: Because you're white.

BRENDA: I'm not white. I'm coloured like you. I'm Black, with a capital B.

DR. BAASA: That is in Britain or America, but not here. Here we have neither caste nor capital divisions, we're all black people.

BRENDA: And that includes me, for I am a citizen of this country.

DR. BAASA: But in your papers you are classed as an Asian in race, and your father had a British passport until last year.

BRENDA: I don't care what the papers say: it is what I feel that matters. And don't forget that my father held a British passport until last year because he couldn't get citizenship without bribing someone. He and his father before him were born here, have lived here all their lives and have done all in their power to show that here is where they really belong. What more could you want? Yet someone insisted on his paying 10,000 shillings, which he refused on principle. All right, after the revolution his services to the country were recognized and your Government granted him citizenship and the Honour of the Spear, which he couldn't refuse because according to custom it would be considered an insult to the giver. You know you can't blame him for having held a British passport until last year. And as for my being classed as Asian by race in my citizenship papers, who is to blame but your Government authorities? Some of the things you put in your forms are more fit for a police state like South Africa.

DR. BAASA: All right, Brenda, you've made your point. But I wouldn't like you to go about thinking I am a racist, if by that term you mean someone who believes either in the extermination or doing down of any other race except his own. I am not a racist but perhaps I am a racialist in that I believe in racial integrity. I believe in live and let live, just as much as I believe in the right of every race to exist: that's the doctor and scientist in me. Maybe time will prove me wrong and in a million years from now it will not be regretted that once upon a time there had been many races of man. As a man and a politician, I believe in the dignity of man, black or white, and in his essential freedom and right to live meaningfully.

BRENDA: And I believe in all these things too.

DR. BAASA: You!

BRENDA: Of course, what do you think?

DR. BAASA: I wouldn't trust you with paint and brush to change the world if I were God. I believe you would paint it as *white* as the *White Cliffs of Dover*. You're such a puritan you should be living in an igloo out in snowland.

BRENDA: Dr Baasa, I'm neither frigid nor stupid enough to believe that brush and paint could change the world. Colour is only skin deep.

DR. BAASA: What? Colour is more than skin deep: it runs in the blood and is the flame of the soul; it is the mask and the shrine of what they call race. If you don't know that, you don't know anything about races.

BRENDA: Marriage between the races is the only solution to such problems.

DR. BAASA: Problem? What problem?

BRENDA: Racial discrimination.

DR. BAASA: Brenda, you can't go about thrusting people into a melting pot just because there's racial discrimination in the world. There will always be another cause for discrimination: look at what is happening in this country between people of different tribes, the prejudices and animosities. Isn't it in some ways worse than racial discrimination? Yet I as Cabinet Minister would be the last to use my power to get us all into a melting pot to create one non-tribal nation. Just as individuals differ, and in this way are more interesting than robots or zombies, so must tribes and races differ. The solution is to realize that these differences should make us value each other, not hate and despise whoever is not like ourselves.

BRENDA: That doesn't preclude marriage.

DR. BAASA: Marriage is between individuals, and it is the individuals themselves who should decide on it on their own. But that doesn't mean that others shouldn't offer advice, parents in particular.

BRENDA: Supposing Jenny were pregnant and had no choice but to get married, what would you advise?

fx: Door opens

JENNY: (*Off mic from door*) Daddy, shall I bring your tea in here?

DR. BAASA: Jenny, come in here a moment, will you?

JENNY: What is it, Daddy?

DR. BAASA: Brenda, what was it you were asking?

JENNY: Please, Daddy, I left the kettle on.

DR. BAASA: Let it boil.

JENNY: I don't want to burn another kettle.

DR. BAASA: Why all this hurry?

JENNY: (*Coming on mic*) All right, what is it? I thought I was intruding.

DR. BAASA: Intruding on what?

JENNY: How should I know?

DR. BAASA: Let's stop going in circles, shall we?

JENNY: Now who is the one going in circles?

DR. BAASA: And don't you answer back my questions with questions.

JENNY: I wish I knew what on earth is upsetting you.

DR. BAASA: I'm not upset.

JENNY: Then why this high and mighty tone? The kettle is boiling now.

DR. BAASA: Jenny, are you all right?

JENNY: What kind of question is that?

DR. BAASA: All right, you can go.

JENNY: (*Going off mic a little*) Thank you, Sir.

DR. BAASA: Jenny, come back.

JENNY: What is it now?

DR. BAASA: Are you pregnant?

JENNY: Why should I be pregnant?

DR. BAASA: I told you not to answer back my questions with questions!

JENNY: Don't shout at me! Why should I be pregnant?

DR. BAASA: You're not?

JENNY: Daddy, if you don't know whom to look out for, it's none of my business to open your eyes.

DR. BAASA: What do you mean?

JENNY: (*Going further off mic*) Ask no questions and you'll be told no lies.

fx: Door slams

BRENDA: Dr Baasa, I only have my suspicions but if this were true –

DR. BAASA: If! For goodness sake, Brenda, can't you be more direct?

BRENDA: I don't want to be proved wrong. What would you do? Would you give them a lecture in racial integrity and prescribe an abortion?

DR. BAASA: You don't know what you're talking about.

BRENDA: I think the world needs people like Jenny and Silva, people who can sacrifice themselves to remind us of the lesson in the rainbow which is made of all the colours.

DR. BAASA: The rainbow is an illusion of light and stray particles in the atmosphere. Perhaps the only true colours are black and white and the rest mere optical illusions. The trouble with you liberals is that you quite often confuse dreams and ideals with reality. You don't seem to realize that often what people say they believe in, and what they actually do, are as contrary as day and night. You want to keep your heads up in the clouds and at the same time you want to keep your feet down on mother earth – you can't have it both ways.

fx: Door opens – sound of trolley with crockery coming towards mic

MRS. BAASA: (*Coming on mic with trolley*) Teatime!

DR. BAASA: I thought Jenny was responsible for tea this afternoon, my dear.

MRS. BAASA: You know how she takes on when shouted at.

DR. BAASA: I didn't shout at her.

MRS. BAASA: I heard your voice out in the garden. Ah, good, here are Mike and Silva now.

MIKE: Come on in, Silva, sit yourself somewhere comfortable.

DR. BAASA: Come and sit here, Silva.

SILVA: (*Coming on mic*) Thank you, Dr Baasa.

MRS. BAASA: How many sugars for you, Silva?

SILVA: Two please, Mrs Baasa.

JENNY: (*Off mic from door*) And two for me, Mama.

MRS. BAASA: But Jenny dear, I thought you were on a diet!

JENNY: (*Coming on mic*) That was last week.

DR. BAASA: Jenny, how is your headache?

JENNY: Who said I had a headache?

DR. BAASA: I thought your mother said you were unwell.

JENNY: Daddy, the only headache I have is you.

MRS. BAASA: Now, Jenny, you can't talk to your father like that.

DR. BAASA: Pardon the lady – she's in love, you know.

MRS. BAASA: In love with what?

DR. BAASA: With whom, you mean. You'll be a grandma before you can say *Zuka*!

MRS. BAASA: I don't believe it!

DR. BAASA: All right, you can wait until you see the baby.

JENNY: Stop it, Daddy, please.

DR. BAASA: Perhaps Silva here can tell us more.

JENNY: I said stop it! I won't have my private affairs discussed in public.

DR. BAASA: Public! You silly idiot, you call this a public meeting?

MRS. BAASA: Now, Danny.

DR. BAASA: Is that the cook you see there? And is the other one the houseboy? And what about these two – are they my friends or yours? Or am I the public you're referring to?

MRS. BAASA: That's enough, Danny.

BRENDA: (*Moving slightly off mic*) I think we ought to be on our way now, Silva.

DR. BAASA: Oh no, you are not going now.

BRENDA: Thank you very much for the tea, Mrs Baasa.

DR. BAASA: You're not leaving this house with empty civilities.

MIKE: Father, please.

DR. BAASA: Did you think this was a game reserve where you could walk in and out as you wish? Did you think we were playing a game of chess with my daughter as a pawn on your liberal chessboard? And you, Silva, have you been messing around with my daughter?

SILVA: Dr Baasa, I will explain –

DR. BAASA: Explain, my foot! Did you tell your father about this affair?

SILVA: No, but –

DR. BAASA: Well, ring him now and tell him. Here, take this
    phone and ring him. You have no guts. You, Brenda, ring
    Dr D'Mello, or I will.

BRENDA: I'm not ringing my father.

DR. BAASA: Do it or I will.

MIKE: Give it to me, father. You heard what she said.

DR. BAASA: You keep out of this.

MIKE: Jenny, tell him it's not true.

JENNY: Not true? But we got married a fortnight ago at the
    City Council.

SILVA: Jenny!

DR. BAASA: What!

MRS. BAASA: Married!

JENNY: It was a false alarm.

SILVA: Jenny, please stop it.

JENNY: I thought I was in trouble.

SILVA: If you won't tell him, I will. Dr Baasa, I'm sorry –

DR. BAASA: Sorry? You've had no cause to be sorry yet.

BRENDA: O God!

DR. BAASA: Just you wait and see.

JENNY: All right, Daddy, I call it off. It was all a joke.

DR. BAASA: You mean – it's not true?

JENNY: Do you think I'm crazy?

BRENDA: O God!

DR. BAASA: You too, Brenda? I thought you were the master-
    mind.

BRENDA: O God!

DR. BAASA: You mean you weren't mixed up in this plot?

BRENDA: Jenny, you tricked me. And Silva, you knew about this
    all morning and all afternoon and you didn't tell me.

DR. BAASA: Isn't anyone going to offer Brenda an apology – or
    me for that matter?

BRENDA: I want more than an apology: I demand a proper
    explanation. You have made a fool of me. The things I have
    said this afternoon, it wasn't a joke, all that.

SILVA: I'm sorry, Brenda, Jenny said not to tell anyone.

BRENDA: For God's sake, Silva, do you have to do everything
    Jenny says?

SILVA: Don't you? (Going off mic) I'll wait for you outside.

MIKE: Wait, Silva, I'm coming too. (Going off mic) Jenny, some
    day your jokes will land you somewhere really nasty.

MRS. BAASA: Jenny, aren't you going to apologize to your friend and to your father?

JENNY: I said it was all a joke.

MRS. BAASA: But that's not an apology!

JENNY: I'm sorry, Dad, you used to have a sense of humour, and I thought you knew me better than that.

DR. BAASA: (*Laughing*) Jenny, the day I hear you apologizing seriously to anyone, I believe I shall die.

JENNY: I hate to kill you now, but I've got to apologize to Brenda.

DR. BAASA: I promise to survive that, she needs it, by God!

JENNY: I'm sorry, Brenda, I hope you learnt something.

DR. BAASA: (*Laughing*) Jenny, you're impossible! I suppose I have to apologize on your behalf, as usual.

MRS. BAASA: Come on and help me clear up.

DR. BAASA: Mary dear, let her clear up and cook the dinner too as a punishment.

MRS. BAASA: You don't want another joke for dinner, do you?

JENNY: (*Going off mic*) Thank you very much.

DR. BAASA: Hey, how about clearing up?

JENNY: (*Off mic from door*) You do it, Mama, please. I'll come and help you in the kitchen later.

MRS. BAASA: Danny, *you* spoilt her.

DR. BAASA: You see, Brenda? All blame eventually comes round to me.

MRS. BAASA: (*Going off mic*) Don't waste your sympathies on him, Brenda, they are all the same – except Mike.

x: Door closes

DR. BAASA: She's right, you know, Mike is the only one in this house with any sense left. The rest of us are just Jenny's puppets. One day he will make some woman really happy.

BRENDA: I feel so exposed.

DR. BAASA: Don't, what we said this afternoon is all confidential.

BRENDA: Thank you.

DR. BAASA: Can I ask you a rather delicate question?

BRENDA: Oh, what about?

DR. BAASA: You and Mike?

BRENDA: I told you, there's nothing going. Must we go into all that again?

DR. BAASA: You're young, Brenda, don't let the prejudices of

F

yesterday influence you unduly. You can get married if you want.

BRENDA: Don't worry, Mike is very safe.

DR. BAASA: I see you haven't forgiven me.

BRENDA: There's nothing to forgive. I believe we know where we stand.

DR. BAASA: Brenda, you know I'm not really opposed to this kind of marriage. I believe that it could be a great experience for the people concerned. But there are problems too which, though not insurmountable, must be faced squarely from the very beginning. This afternoon you've made me feel that you could make a success of such a marriage. I would love to see you marry Mike.

BRENDA: But Dr Baasa, the things I said were just for argument!

DR. BAASA: You mean you don't believe them?

BRENDA: In principle, yes, but I haven't thought of doing them myself.

DR. BAASA: Well, why not give it a chance? Anyone can see that Mike is very fond of you.

BRENDA: It takes two to make an affair –

DR. BAASA You like him now, why shouldn't you grow to love him in time?

BRENDA: My father wouldn't approve.

DR. BAASA: Leave that to me, I'll have a word with him at the National Convention next week.

BRENDA: Please don't – he will kill me!

DR. BAASA: Nonsense, Dr D'Mello has been a great friend of mine for years now.

BRENDA: You don't understand.

DR. BAASA: Besides, I believe he thinks very well of Mike.

BRENDA: I can't marry Mike, I've told you.

DR. BAASA: Why, because he's not Asian like you?

BRENDA: It's not that.

DR. BAASA: Well, what is it then? Isn't he handsome enough or bright enough?

BRENDA: You're not being fair. Didn't you say yourself that marriage is between individuals and that they themselves should decide on it on their own?

DR. BAASA: All right, are you going to do that? Are you going to give Mike a chance?

fx: Door opens

MIKE: (*Off mic from door*) Are you through now?

DR. BAASA: Oh, Mike, come in.

MIKE: (*Coming in on mic*) What is it, father?

DR. BAASA: Shall we make a proposal?

MIKE: What proposal?

BRENDA: Dr Baasa, please stop!

DR. BAASA: Oblige the young lady, Mike. Don't you want to get married?

MIKE: Married? Father, I'm doing my finals next year and after that there's internship, after which I hope to go abroad for further studies.

DR. BAASA: Does that mean you won't think of marriage until you're forty?

MIKE: Are you asking me to propose to Brenda?

DR. BAASA: Well, why not.

MIKE: Brenda, would you marry me?

DR. BAASA: No conditions, be direct.

MIKE: Okay – will you marry me?

BRENDA: No, Mike, he can't tell you what to do.

MIKE: He's not telling me, I'm asking you.

BRENDA: You're not serious – so stop embarrassing me!

MIKE: Oh, am I embarrassing you?

BRENDA: You know I'm fond of you, but I don't want to marry you.

MIKE: Why?

BRENDA: How can I explain what I don't know myself?

MIKE: But if you're fond of me –

BRENDA: Even if I loved you –

MIKE: You wouldn't marry me?

BRENDA: Please, Dr Baasa, I'm sorry. I know you must think I am a liar.

DR. BAASA: No – just a hypocrite.

Full-Cycle

GORDON TIALOBI

Gordon Tialobi, *born in Warri in 1940, was educated there before going to London in 1963.* Full-Cycle *was his first radio play and is the first of his work to be published. He also translates work from Yoruba, and a collection of his translations of Yoruba poetry is due to be published at the end of 1972. He has acted in many* African Theatre *productions, and also works as a designer and sculptor.*

Recorded Sunday 7th March 1971

CAST
Maga – Bloke Modisane
Mrs Maga – Rakie Mukhtar
Man – Alton Kumalo
Girl– Musindo Mwinyipembe
Usher – Willie Jonah
Judge – Cosmo Pieterse

SOUND EFFECTS
Alarm clock
Gun shot
Wooden hammer
Chair
Door

fx: Fade in the noise of snoring, the loud ticking of a clock which persists throughout the play. There is a sudden noise off mic, as of a chair being bumped into. The sound of snoring stops abruptly

MAGA: (*Alarmed*) Who's there? . . . Who's there?

MAN: Don't move – and don't make a noise. We've got guns, and we can see you clearly. So, don't make a noise . . . Now, slowly reach out for your bed-switch, and switch on the light – slowly . . . slowly . . .

fx: Light switch click

MAN: That's better.

GIRL: Get out of that bed.

MAGA: What!

GIRL: You heard. I said get out!

MAN: I haven't got anything on except my pants.

GIRL: And I don't care if you haven't got your pants on, either. Get out.

MAN: Hold your hands up high, and move slowly . . .

MAGA: For heaven's sake, what's this about? What d'you want?

MAN: Where's your uniform?

MAGA: What uniform?

MAN: Your General's uniform.

GIRL: We're taking you to your trial.

MAGA: My trial! . . . You're joking.

MAN: Oh no, we're not.

MAGA: This is ridiculous. I'm not going anywhere. I'm not going to any trial.

MAN: All right, if that's the way you want it –

MAGA: What are you doing? . . . No! Please don't. Don't.

fx: A shot is fired

MAN: (*With mock disappointment*) Missed! I sometimes miss my first shot . . . but *never* the second. Are you coming or not? Do we have to take you dead or alive?

MAGA: Oh my God! You're mad.

MAN: For the last time, are you coming with us dead or alive?

MAGA: Yes, I'm coming.

GIRL: Dead or alive?

MAGA: Alive.

GIRL: That's more like it. Now, where's your uniform?

MAGA: In that wardrobe . . .

MAN: I like the . . . (*rhyming with the clock's movement*) tick-tock

tick-tock tick-tock of your table clock . . . It's so clean, so
clear . . .

GIRL: (*Coming in on mic*) The Court must be impatient by now.
Put them on. Hurry.

MAN: . . . Yes, I think you made the right decision – I mean,
choosing to come with us alive.

MAGA: You mean I had a choice?

MAN: I suppose that's another way of looking at it.

MAGA: Oh my God, this can't be true – I must be dreaming.
Who are you, what do you want with me?

MAN: As to your first question, yes, this is real all right. Who we
are, and what we are, you'll soon find out.

MAGA: What am I supposed to have done? I haven't done
anything. What have I done?

MAN: You are to be tried for war crimes –

GIRL: Murders, rapes, looting and all other crimes committed by
you during the war . . .

MAGA: I didn't –

GIRL: Or under your command.

MAGA: What war are you talking about?

GIRL: The last civil war.

MAGA: But the war ended years ago . . . You're mad. You're
both mad.

MAN: The war may have ended years ago, but we haven't
forgotten.

MAGA: Listen, I did nothing wrong during the war. I did my
best. I did what I believed to be right –

GIRL: Did you hear that? He has admitted guilt.

MAGA: I haven't admitted anything. Look, if this is somebody's
idea of a practical joke, let's put a stop to it right now. This
is a joke, isn't it? . . . Look, I have long since retired from
public life – I lead a quiet life here in my village. I haven't
done anything.

MAN: Save your breath for the Court.

GIRL: You'll need it.

MAGA: I want my lawyer.

GIRL: We've got one for you.

MAGA: I want my own lawyer.

MAN: Are you going to start arguing with us again?

MAGA: If I'm being tried, then I want to be represented by my
own lawyer.

GIRL: I think he has changed his mind. I think he now wishes to
    be taken there dead.

MAN: Oh well, if that's the way you want it . . .

MAGA: (*In a terrified voice*) No! Please don't . . . whatever you say
    . . . I want your lawyer, I don't want my lawyer . . .

MAN: That's better. Come on, let's go . . . (*Off mic*) Hold on a
    sec . . . (*Coming on mic*) That clock – I like that clock. (*Fade
    up clock ticks*) . . . I know, I want you to wear it on your belt
    for me . . .

Fade out

Fade in

*fx: Noise of crowd. Shouts of 'hang Maga', 'shoot him', 'death to Maga',
    etc.*

MAN: (*As if fighting through the crowd*) Stand back . . . Stand back
    everyone . . . Let him through . . .

fx: Door shuts, cut out crowd noise

MAN: Phew, that was close!

GIRL: I wouldn't say they were particularly friendly, would you,
    Maga?

MAN: Of course you wouldn't. That's why your trial is in camera,
    private.

GIRL: (*With a giggle*) After all, we want you too.

MAGA: I demand a public hearing.

GIRL: Demand! Demand is a strong word. Aren't you forgetting
    who you are –

MAN: And where you are? Before this Supreme Court, everybody
    is nothing. And that includes you.

MAGA: What Supreme Court –

GIRL: Only that in your case, you're lucky to be told you are
    even equal to nothing, considering your crimes.

MAGA: What crimes? I'm not guilty of any crimes.

GIRL: Murders, rapes, lootings and all other crimes.

MAGA: For Heaven's sake, this is crazy. Who are you? What do
    you want? Where am I?

JUDGE: (*Off mic as outside door*) Bring in the criminal!

fx: Door opens

USHER: (*Shouting*) Bring in the criminal . . (*Coming on mic from
    door*) Oh, there you are . . . (*In a military voice*) Attention:

General Maga, that command was for you. In future, I shall
not repeat myself. You must consider yourself a soldier once
again, and one more military disobedience like that and
you'll be shot on the spot. Now, let's try again . . .
Attention! . . . That's better. Left turn! . . . By the left,
forward march, one two, one two, one two, one two, halt!
Left turn! Right about turn! Stand at ease! Easy . . . Your
Honour, the criminal, General Maga . . .

fx: Door shuts

JUDGE: Is your name Criminal General Maga?

MAGA: General Maga, Your Honour, not Criminal General
Maga.

USHER: (*In military style*) Criminal, attention! Right turn! By the
left, forward march . . .

JUDGE: Just a minute, just a minute . . . Where are you going?

USHER: Outside, sir, Your Honour, to shoot him, teach him a
lesson, never to contradict Your Honour.

JUDGE: Mr Usher, if you don't mind, I can run this Court
myself, thank you. Bring the criminal back.

USHER: As you wish, Your Honour, sir . . . Back to your former
position, on the double . . .

JUDGE: Criminal General Maga, I'm sorry to call you Criminal
General Maga, but according to these memos and documents
here, that's your name, and that's final. If the name feels a
bit strange at the moment, don't worry, you'll soon get used
to it. At this juncture, let me warn you I have not much
power over this Court or its happenings. I just follow the
course of history. Today, you're going to be part of history.
Today or tomorrow – who cares. I see by the clock you are
wearing that you are an expert on this subject, so let it pass,
and let history take its course. But before we proceed any
further, have you anything to say?

MAGA: Have I anything to say? Thousands – millions –

GIRL: Your Honour, I submit that these lunatic ravings have no
bearings on the issue at hand. I beg Your Honour to listen to
his heart, and to the patriotic clamour outside, and let justice
be done.

JUDGE: Having allowed him to say millions, I am half inclined
to agree with you. But, let us be generous. Let us give him
another chance. Have you anything more to say?

MAGA: Jesus Christ! Where am I? Who are you? What do you want? Why am I here? Who are you?

JUDGE: Please, please . . . a few questions at a time . . . As to where you are, you are in the Supreme Court for War Criminals –

MAGA: A Supreme Court! How can you call this a Court, with only five of us present in this make-shift room?

JUDGE: We decided not to waste the taxpayers' money on those embellishments you seem to want. We are already spending quite a lot as it is.

MAGA: I was told I had a Defence Counsel. Where is he?

JUDGE: He is prosecuting – as you must have gathered by now – and she is your Defence Counsel.

GIRL: Your Honour, with your permission, we've decided to switch roles. I am now prosecuting.

MAGA: You! Him! Somebody help me – I'm going mad. I mean, this can't be true – it can't be happening. (*Shouting*) Let me out of here!

JUDGE: Silence in Court.

USHER: You there, silence in Court.

JUDGE: Mr Defence Counsel, you had better restrain your client from another outburst like that or I shall really blow my top.

MAN: Yes, Your Honour, I shall speak to him . . . What did you go and do that for? I mean, is there any sense in wanting to get out of here? I mean, look at the crowd waiting for you outside. Why don't you try to be brave, see things as they are? Believe me, you are safest in here.

MAGA: I'm mad, I'm sure I'm mad. Things like this don't happen. I must be mad.

MAN: Your Honour, my client pleads insanity.

MAGA: What!

MAN: (*Trying to hush Maga*) That's what you said just now, isn't it? You said –

JUDGE: In any case, according to these documents before me, I am forced to reject your plea as premature. I have before me a set of standard routines and sub-routines, and the criminal does not enter his plea until we have reached . . .

fx: Rifling through papers

. . . Yes, until we have reached the item where I ask: 'Criminal General Maga, what is your plea, are you guilty or not guilty?', and the next item after that is 'I hereby senten–' . . . blah blah blah, etc. etc. Meanwhile, where am I? . . . Oh yes, 'Call the first witness'.

USHER: *(Calling)* Call the first witness! Call the first witne– . . . *(with a chuckle)* Ah, Your Honour, I'm the first witness.

MAGA: You!

USHER: Serjeant-Major Bondo, formerly of the 7th Paratroop Brigade.

JUDGE: Get on with it.

GIRL: Tell the Court, in your own words, what you have to say.

USHER: In my own words . . . yes . . . well . . . er, which accusation do you want first?

GIRL: Choose any.

USHER: Well, er, there's this one – oh it's a good one. Well, this day, I briefed my men we were to take paratroop action against an enemy enclave –

GIRL: And where was this enemy enclave?

USHER: Thirty-five miles due north-north-east . . . *(Lapsing)* or was it north-north-west . . .

JUDGE: Of where?

USHER: Of the demilitarized zone.

JUDGE: Well, which was it?

USHER: Which was what?

JUDGE: Which was it, north-north-west or north-north-east?

USHER: Well, that was it, sir. After we were airborne, I forgot whether it was north-north-east or north-north-west. Before becoming airborne, I had previously destroyed all documents pertinent to this action – military tactics, Your Honour, read and destroy. Where was I? . . . Having discovered my dilemma, I duly tossed a coin, and it came up tails, and that was what I had chosen for north-north-west . . .

JUDGE: Well? . . .

USHER: It was a calamity, sir. 35 miles north-north-west of the demilitarized zone led straight to my village. *(Trying to work up some emotional agitation)* Wiped out, it was, everybody, everything that moved, that flew, that swam, that –

MAN: Wait a minute, you mean you went fishing on that mission?

GIRL: What's that got to do with it?

MAN: Well, if it's true he destroyed everything that swam, it goes without saying, therefore, that he went fishing on a mission, contrary to regulations –

GIRL: Red herring, Your Honour – absolute red herring – a blatant attempt to divert the attention of the Court from the serious issues at hand, that my client was made to wipe out his village –

USHER: And my mother!

GIRL: And his mother –

USHER: And my favourite goat!

GIRL: And his favourite goat. I submit, Your Honour, that these crimes must not go unpunished with impunity. I therefore demand the death penalty.

JUDGE: Miss Prosecutor, let me say here and now that I admire your strong sense of involvement. I can see you know your business and what it is all about. There are not many people like that around these days, so I commend you . . . Criminal General Maga, have you anything to add to that?

MAGA: (*Despairingly*) Nothing. You're all mad, all of you, mad.

GIRL: Contempt of Court. Your Honour, this is contempt of Court

JUDGE: Mr Defence Counsel, I would like to remind you that in my Court, there is a hundred per cent freedom of speech. Let me therefore warn you that one more outburst like that and I should hand him over to the mob outside. I mean that.

MAGA: Would someone please explain to me what all this has got to do with me?

GIRL: Really, General Maga, you are not trying to disclaim your responsibilities as a soldier?

MAGA: Let me understand one thing at least; am I being charged because he wiped out his village?

GIRL: What do you think?

MAGA: I don't know, that's why I'm asking.

GIRL: Hazard a guess.

MAGA: Because I've never met this man before. He never served under me. If he made a mistake and wiped out his village, why should I be made to answer for it? It's got nothing to do with me –

USHER: (*Breaking down and crying*) My mother . . . Oh, my dear mother . . . My poor, dear mother . . .

MAGA: I had nothing to do with it.

GIRL: Your Honour, the accused admits he is guilty –

MAN: Yes, but we've already pleaded insanity.

GIRL: That's not enough.

MAN: All right, if you're not satisfied, we'll throw in diminished responsibility due to senility. There, that should make you happy. How about it?

MAGA: Look, I don't know what you people are trying to do to me, but you are almost succeeding in driving me out of my mind. Won't somebody please say something that makes sense? I can't stand this much longer. Please, say something, do something that makes sense . . . please . . .

JUDGE: Well, as I said before, Mr Defence Counsel, you cannot enter your plea, or any plea, for that matter, until I ask you to. So, I hereby reject your plea . . . Call the next witness.

USHER: Call the next witness! Call the – . . . Er, Your Honour, I'm the next witness.

JUDGE: You again?

USHER: Nothing personal, Your Honour, it's just that, well, there's another incident.

MAGA: 35 miles north-north-east or west this time?

General uproar in which everybody starts shouting at each other, all talking at the same time

GIRL: . . . Your Honour, this is contempt. You mustn't let this go unpunished. You must do something . . .

USHER: . . . How dare you interrupt me while I'm talking? How dare you . . .

MAN: My client has a right to exercise his freedom of speech. Freedom of speech . . .

MAGA: This is no Court, this is a mad house . . . You're all mad . . . You're all insane . . .

JUDGE: . . . Temper . . . temper . . . I want everybody to keep his cool . . .

After a while, the Judge shouts above the din

Silence! . . . Silence in my Court.

FX: *Bang of judge's hammer*

USHER: (*Taking up the call*) Silence in Court!

JUDGE: (*Angry*) Thank you . . . Now, I want absolute silence in this Court as from now on. One more upheaval like this and I shall clear this Court . . . Second witness, take the stand.

USHER: Yes, Your Honour.

JUDGE: Now, do you swear to tell the truth, the whole truth, and nothing but the truth?

USHER: I swear.

JUDGE: Then, get on with it.

USHER: First of all, in answer to his question, the answer –

MAN: And which question is that?

USHER: You know – whether it was north-north-east or north-north-west. The answer is neither . . . Actually, (*Suddenly becoming convivial*) this incident is recent – last week – when I applied for this job as an usher.

MAGA: (*In exasperation*) I thought I was being tried for war crimes?

MAN: What my client is trying to say is that he wishes this new evidence to be classified as military.

GIRL: Your Honour, the Prosecution objects to this new shift of emphasis as irrelevant.

JUDGE: Objection sustained. Will the defence please shift from the irrelevant to the relevant.

MAN: We'll stick to Your Honour's ruling, much as it saddens us.

JUDGE: Good. Proceed, second witness.

USHER: After the war, Your Honour, I was declared redundant and demobilized. No work, sir. Cut off, just like that. No means to support my three wives and thirteen children. It was cruel –

GIRL: Yes, well, tell us what you did during your unemployment.

USHER: Scrounged, Madam. Lived off people. Took what they gave me, or what I took for granted they gave me . . . Took what I found, and what I took for granted they wanted me to find.

JUDGE: Could you elaborate more explicitly. It is beginning to sound as if what you are trying to tell the Court is that you are a thief.

USHER: That's a matter of opinion, Your Honour.

JUDGE: Then it is my opinion that you were a thief.

USHER: No sir, I'd say I lived a life based on the philosophy of 'Finders Keepers!'

JUDGE: Nonsense, nonsense.

USHER: All right, if that's the way you feel about it, then I will proceed with my evidence . . . Where was I? . . . Yes, it's like this, Your Honour. When I applied for this job, I was told I could have it for a fifty-pound bribe.

GIRL: Only fifty pounds, did you say?

USHER: Yes.

GIRL: Didn't you think it odd, at the time, that they should only want fifty pounds for such a secure, posh job?

USHER: Yes . . . There must be a catch somewhere, I said to myself, there is a catch – there must be a catch.

GIRL: And was there a catch?

USHER: Oh yes, there was.

GIRL: And what was it.

USHER: I can't repeat it, Your Honour. It had to do with my family honour.

GIRL: You mean it had to do with your seventeen-year-old daughter?

USHER: (*Coyly*) Yes.

General reaction from all

JUDGE: Silence in Court!

USHER: Silence in Court!

JUDGE: That's better. Let us keep it that way.

MAGA: (*Wearily*) Your Honour, please, may I say something?

JUDGE: Sure. It's your trial.

MAGA: I've been listening to you, and I keep telling myself this is a practical joke . . . Only, somehow, I don't think it is . . . Why me? What have I done? What have I got to do with any of these accusations? Somebody please tell me . . .

USHER: May I answer his question? Because it strikes me where it hurts most. You see, during the war, I wiped out my entire village. Never mind if it was my fault or not. The fact is that I did it for the war. And why? Because you people said it was to free us from political oppressors and tyrants, corruption and bribery, tribalism, nepotism – name it, you said it. And what happens after the war? Whereas I could have had this job for fifty pounds and my seventeen-year-old daughter thrown in, in fact, now I have to add my thirteen-year-old girl as well . . .

General reaction from all

JUDGE: Silence in Court!

USHER: Silence in Court!

JUDGE: Did you mention your thirteen-year-old daughter?

USHER: I most certainly did.

JUDGE: Well, in the light of this new evidence, I have no choice
but to hear the case in camera. I therefore declare the Court
adjourned. I shall see the witness in my chamber.

USHER: All rise . . .

JUDGE: (*Going off mic towards door*) Now, tell me, Mr Usher, you
say your thirteen-year-old daughter is involved in . . .

MAGA: This can't be true.

MAN: Don't despair yet. The prosecution's case may not be as
damnable as it appears.

MAGA: This can't be happening. I mean, I must be mad.

MAN: Well, we've already entered that plea, and quite frankly,
I think it's going to fail.

MAGA: For Christ's sake, who are you? What do you want?

MAN: Don't be distraught. It's not the end of the way, you know.
I mean, anything can happen. Look, we've got your wife
outside, waiting to come in and cheer you up. How about
that? We'll give you all the privacy you want. We'll even
open the back door –

we'll open the back door to let in some fresh air. (*Going off
mic*) How about that? . . . Ah, I see you like that. Come on,
everybody out . . .

fx: Door opens

MAN: (*Off mic as from outside door*) You can go in now, Mrs
Maga . . .

MRS. MAGA: (*Anxiously running from door in on mic*) Are you all
right? Are you all right?

MAGA: I'm fine – how about you? Are you all right?

MRS. MAGA: I'm at my wits' end. What is happening?

MAGA: I wish I knew . . . I've been thinking . . . I have a feeling
we've been kidnapped by some madmen.

MRS. MAGA: Kidnapped by madmen? Oh, my God.

MAGA: I can't think of any other explanation for this . . .
madness.

MRS. MAGA: What are we going to do?

MAGA: Get out, one way or another . . . Look, the back door is
open! Come on, let's go.

MRS. MAGA: Don't! I heard them posting some guards outside it.
They have orders to shoot to kill if you try to escape . . .

MAGA: Why us, I keep asking myself?

MRS. MAGA: I think we'd better humour them – play along with them, and . . .

MAGA: Humour them? I'm so confused I don't know if they are humouring me or not . . . How did they get you?

MRS. MAGA: I heard a noise downstairs, and I thought a window was open. I went down to close it, and they were there . . . What are we going to do?

MAGA: You'll be all right. I think it's me they want.

MRS. MAGA: They'll have to have me too. I'm not leaving you.

MAGA: Be sensible –

MRS. MAGA: Besides, if they don't want me, why are they trying me for complicity?

MAGA: Trying you! You mean they are trying you? For complicity? In what?

fx: There is a knock, the door opens

GIRL: (*Coming on mic from door*) I'm sorry, Mrs Maga, but you have to leave now.

MRS. MAGA: I'm not leaving, I'm staying with my husband.

GIRL: Come, come, Mrs Maga, don't be difficult.

MRS. MAGA: I'm not leaving.

MAN: Oh yes, you are.

MRS. MAGA: (*Screaming as pulled away off mic to door*) Leave me alone! I want to stay with my husband. Leave me alone . . .

MAN: (*Shouting after her*) Don't worry, Mrs Maga, we'll take care of your husband . . .

As her screams go off, the Judge's laughter comes in on mic

JUDGE: (*Laughing*) That was very funny . . . Very funny. Ha ha ha.

USHER: I'm glad you enjoyed it, Your Honour.

JUDGE: Oh, I enjoyed it.

USHER: Thank you, Your Honour . . . (*Announcing him*) All stand!

JUDGE: Yes, I've heard the evidence of the second witness. Very funny . . . (*Clears his throat and tries to be serious*) Call the third witness.

USHER: Call the third witness!

GIRL: Your Honour, I'm the third witness.

JUDGE: Isn't that a bit irregular?

GIRL: Not at all, Your Honour, it's done every day.

JUDGE: Really?

GIRL: Do you remember the film, *The Lady from Shanghai* by Orson Welles?

JUDGE: No, I can't say I do.

GIRL: Well, there's this Defence Counsel who testifies and cross-examines himself in it.

JUDGE: Are you saying it was done by Orson Welles?

GIRL: Absolutely.

JUDGE: If it was done by Orson Welles, then it must be right. I have that much faith in him. Step on the witness stand.

GIRL: Do I promise to tell the truth, the whole truth, and nothing but the truth? . . . I do . . . What are my charges? My charges are, that my husband died in the war. Full stop.

JUDGE: You can't have a full stop yet. You've just started.

GIRL: But that's all, Your Honour.

JUDGE: No, no. Cross-examine yourself, and tell the Court why we should find Maga guilty.

GIRL: I see what you mean. Well, to come to the point quickly, I accuse General Maga of depriving me of my wifely securities.

JUDGE: Such as . . .

GIRL: Such as . . . well, for example, every Saturday, my husband used to play the record 'Everybody Likes Saturday Night'.

JUDGE: 'Everybody Likes Saturday Night' . . . Never heard of it.

GIRL: It's a beautiful tune (*Starts to sing it*)
          Everybody likes Saturday night,
          Everybody likes Saturday night,
          Everybody, everybody, everybody . . .

MAN: Oh, I know it . . . (*Joining in*)
          Everybody likes Saturday night . . .

USHER: (*Also joining in*) Everybody likes Saturday night . . .

JUDGE: (*Excited*) I know it, I know it . . . (*He joins in and takes the lead*) . . . Come on, everybody, join in the song . . .
     Usher and man join in the chorus, clapping and stamping

MAGA: . . . Stop it! Stop it! . . . I can't stand it any longer . . . Who are you? . . . What do you want? Please tell me, someone . . . Someone please tell me.

JUDGE: Steady on. You know who we are, and where we are. As for your not being able to stand it any longer, it is manifestly

clear your mind is not what it should be. The Court is
already aware of that, so relax.

MAGA: What are you trying to do to me?

JUDGE: We are trying to try you and, if guilty, sentence you.

MAGA: What if I'm innocent?

JUDGE: We'll have to wait and see.

GIRL: Anyway, you're guilty, so the question of your innocence
doesn't arise.

MAN: You are not the only man who has got a good case, you
know. Ours is almost as good.

JUDGE: I shall not tolerate any bickerings in my Court. Will the
witness please continue with her testimony. And as from –

USHER: Silence in Court!

JUDGE: I beg your pardon!

USHER: With no disrespect, Your Honour, I think this hearing
has dragged on long enough, and I now want it to end,
finish . . . sabi?

JUDGE: Well, of all the impudence!

USHER: Impudence nothing. I have a feeling you're forgetting
who you are, and where you are, and who put you there.

JUDGE: Oh, I'm sorry.

USHER: So you should be. By my stop watch, I was supposed to
have taken over from you five minutes ago.

JUDGE: All right, all right, whatever you say.

USHER: Right – take him away!

MAGA: (*Protesting*) I am innocent. I haven't done anything. I am
innocent . . .

USHER: Take him outside and stand him by the wall.

MAGA: (*Being pushed off mic to door*) I am innocent, I am
innocent . . .

fx: Sounds of struggle. Door opens. Noise of crowd shouting

USHER: (*Shouting*) And somebody get me that clock he's wearing
on his belt . . .

fx: Clock's tick

Maga! Have you any last wish?

MAGA: (*From off mic outside*) I haven't done anything. I am
innocent of all your accusations. This is cold-blooded . . .

USHER: Sergeant, I hope your platoon knows the drill. The first
signal is for the platoon to take position and aim. The second

signal is for the drum roll and the gong beat. And on the third beat of the gong, fire! . . . All right, here we go . . . Drums! . . .

fx: Drum roll

USHER: . . . Gongs! . . .

fx: Three gongs beat – on third beat shots fired

Cross fade to

fx: Morning sounds – alarm clock is ringing

MRS. MAGA: (*Coming in on mic from door*) Wake up, Maga. Are you all right? . . . Wake up . . .

fx: Clock stops ringing

MAGA: (*Still protesting*) No! . . . Don't! I'm innocent . . . (*Waking up*) What – where am I? What's happening? . . .

MRS. MAGA: It's all right . . . I think you've been having a bad dream. You were groaning in your sleep . . .

MAGA: I thought I was dead for a minute . . .

MRS. MAGA: It is a beautiful morning, and you're not dead . . . and you're still my husband.

MAGA: (*Teasing her*) Perhaps we're both dead and we don't know it.

MRS. MAGA: All right, if we are both dead, then you shouldn't feel hungry. Do you want your breakfast or not?

MAGA: Mmm, ask me again after breakfast.

MRS. MAGA: Do you want to get up now?

MAGA: I think I'll just lie back a bit and yawn a few more times.

MRS. MAGA: Shall I draw the curtains?

MAGA: Er, no – leave them for now . . .

fx: There is a noise off mic in distance

What's that?

MRS. MAGA: Kitchen window. Must have left it open . . .

fx: There is another noise off mic

MRS. MAGA: I think I had better go and shut it . . . Well, (*Moving off mic to door*) you can lie back – but only for a few minutes . . .

MAGA: This clock ticks too loud.

MRS. MAGA: What?
MAGA: Nothing . . .

*fx: Door shuts . . . there are one or two yawns, followed by snores.
There is a sudden noise off mic, as of a chair being bumped into.
The snoring stops abruptly*

MAGA: (*Alarmed*) Who's there? . . . Who's there?
MAN: (*Sternly*) Don't move – and don't make a noise. We've got
guns, and we can see you clearly. So, don't make a noise . . .
Now, slowly reach out for your bed-switch, and switch on
the light – slowly . . . slowly . . .

x : Light switch click

That's better.
GIRL: Get out of that bed.
MAGA: What!
GIRL: You heard. I said get out!
MAGA: I haven't got anything on except my pants.
GIRL: And I don't care if you haven't got your pants on, either.
Get out . . .

Fade out

Company Pot
A Concert Party Performance

PATIENCE HENAKU ADDO

Patience Henaku Addo, *born in Ghana, was educated at Achimota School. After training as a teacher she took the Diploma Course in Drama and Theatre Studies at the University of Ghana, Legon, and then did a Post-Graduate Certificate course for Teachers of Drama at Bristol University. She has taught in Middle and Secondary Schools in Accra, when she was able to work in educational drama and traditional dance, two of her major areas of interest. She has had poetry in Twi and in English published in Ghanaian magazines. In 1971 she directed another of her plays in Bristol, where she is now living with her husband.*
Recorded 5th March 1972

CAST
Akyebi B – Jumoke Debaye
Pamonie – Yemi Ajibade
Lovelace – Rudolph Walker
Akye – Jeillo Edwards
A plain-clothes policeman – Alex Tetteh-Lartey
An advertiser – Rudolph Walker
Other parts played by members of the cast

SOUND EFFECTS
Street noises
Handbell
Highlife music
Music as from musical box
Door

Author's Note
The style of this play owes something to the Concert Parties which have evolved in Ghana since the War.

fx: Fade up street atmosphere – highlife music – fade under, as hand bell rung

ADVERTISER: (*Coming on mic*) O Charlie – o, O Charlie – o!
O Charlie – o, O Charlie – o!
O Charlie – o, O Charlie – o!
O Charlie – o, O Charlie – o!
O Charlie – o, O Charlie – o!
Twinkle Stars! Twinkle Stars special! Twinkle Stars Concert
Party storming this town tonight. Dua Nkontompo, two
Nnabraba Special! Okukuseku Promotions! (*Going off mic*)
Come one, come all.
O Charlie – o, O Charlie – o.

fx: Peak atmosphere and highlife music – hold – then fade under and lose music gradually

AKYEBI: (*Coming on mic*) Men and women of this town, greetings.
It has been difficult for me to get a job. Difficult. Not that
I didn't hear it when the school bell rang. I did. And went,
but at Middle Form One I had to stop. Awo my mother said
there was no money to pay my fees. So it has been really
difficult to find a job. Not that serving in a bar is not work.
It is. But I would do better with something else, a regular
job. And I have no vocation. Again I would need money to
pay for it if I want to train in one. And there is no money; I
could do better with something else. If . . . er . . . if any man
could employ me in his house . . . permanently . . . keep me
comfortably. But usefully . . . yes, usefully . . . happily . . .
that would be best. Meanwhile I am a bar girl . . . as I said,
at Ahope Bar. I do not mind not being given a trial, not
forgetting that I must eat, clothe myself, pay rent and enjoy
myself. This is the door of my small room – by the way my
name is Beauty Akyebi. Auntie B. So, young men, over to
you.

fx: Peak up street noises – fade under

AKYEBI: Now, where is my key?
PAMONIE: Excuse me, miss.
AKYEBI: Hello. This is my room. What do you want here?
PAMONIE: What do I want here?
AKYEBI: Yes, what are you doing here?

PAMONIE: Looking for you, of course.

AKYEBI: (*Giggling*) Oh.

PAMONIE: I saw you at Ahope Bar last night, didn't I?

AKYEBI: (*Pretending to be thinking*) Er . . . I think you did.

PAMONIE: And said I would see you later, but I didn't realize I
would see you looking so smart in your cloth.

AKYEBI: Oh. You said you would see me later, did you?

PAMONIE: And talk to you.

AKYEBI: Well . . . I am listening.

PAMONIE: Miss B!

AKYEBI: Yeees.

PAMONIE: I . . .

AKYEBI: *E . . . heeee?*

PAMONIE: I want to . . . do with you.

AKYEBI: (*Not shocked*) You want to what?

PAMONIE: Do with you.

AKYEBI: Do with me?

PAMONIE: That's right. (*Pronounced 'Daasraet'*)

AKYEBI: Do what with me?

PAMONIE: Oh . . . I mean . . . You are a woman, aren't you?

AKYEBI: Hm – m – m.

PAMONIE: Unmarried, not so?

AKYEBI: Well . . . so.

PAMONIE: That's right. (*Pronounced 'Daasraet'*) So I want to try
. . . with you . . . like man and woman. When boy meets
girl . . .

AKYEBI: Oh – but you can't be a boy. I may be a girl.

PAMONIE: It doesn't make any difference.

AKYEBI: Listen, I need some time to think about it.

PAMONIE: I shall give you time to think about it carefully.

AKYEBI: To make up my mind. It takes time.

PAMONIE: Er . . . may I ask . . . How long?

Pause

AKYEBI: Oh! . . . Oh! (*As if suddenly remembering something*) I
think I saw you. Ha. (*As if in doubt*) Didn't you park your
Volkswagen in the yard?

PAMONIE: A blue Volkswagen, you mean?

AKYEBI: *E-hee.*

PAMONIE: The other car, usually parked in front of your
manager's garage – that's mine. A 220S.

AKYEBI: (*Eyes open wide*) The black Benz?

PAMONIE: Hm – m – m.

AKYEBI: It has a wireless aerial?

PAMONIE: Yes. Also fitted with a record player.

AKYEBI: Ei! . . . super! Er . . . Mr. . . .

PAMONIE: Pamonie.

AKYEBI: Yes . . . Mr Pamonie, didn't you come to our place
   last Saturday night with your wife?

PAMONIE: Wife? (*Thinking*) I never . . . could it be . . . what did
   this woman look like?

AKYEBI: Sort of tall and . . . in fact, she was in the car, and
   looks like she . . . er . . . uses Dorot. And her hair is dyed
   brown.

PAMONIE: Oh, she! She had a message from my friend for me.

AKYEBI: A message?

PAMONIE: And a parcel from my friend. In fact we were meeting
   this same friend there.

AKYEBI: You are not also a farmer, are you? I mean you do not
   run a farm with this friend?

PAMONIE: Not a farm. We run some other business together.
   Otherwise I am an agent for a Syrian firm.

AKYEBI: Hmm. All right. (*Pause*) Mr Pamonie.

PAMONIE: Yes?

AKYEBI: I shall ask you another question.

PAMONIE: Do.

AKYEBI: Why do you follow me to my house?

PAMONIE: Because I like you.

AKYEBI: And why do you like me?

PAMONIE: You are pretty.

AKYEBI: Oh. (*She is shy*) Is that all?

PAMONIE: There are other things. Here.

fx: Rustle of paper money

   Some business awaits me. That's for pocket money.

AKYEBI: What? . . . A ten cedi note . . . why?

PAMONIE: (*Going off mic*) I'll see you again tomorrow morning,
   with some things for your room. Bye bye.

AKYEBI: (*Stunned*) Ei! Is that what life in this town is? I haven't
   even agreed to be his friend and . . . it looks like he is a
   married man. I am not going to get involved with him. (*To
   audience*) Elderly men and women, you won't advise me to

use this money, would you? I suppose if I do, the next time
he comes I shall find it difficult to turn him out. Well – I'd
better get into my small room.

fx: Door unlocks – opens

LOVELACE: (*Sings off mike*)

AKYEBI: Is that a beggar singing? Let him keep his troubles to
himself! What did Mr Pamonie say? Sounds like he wants a
woman to marry? (*Pause*) Well . . . It is work that I am
looking for . . . a job. But if he marries me, I guess I shall be
taken care of. I shall be secure at least.

fx: Bring up street noises – singing closer

AKYEBI: Awura – your song is too loud.

LOVELACE: Er . . . Ewuraba. Excuse me Ewuraba . . .

AKYEBI: Are you speaking to me?

LOVELACE: Do you happen to know the pretty woman who
serves at Ahope Bar?

AKYEBI: Her name?

LOVELACE: Can't remember. But I . . .

AKYEBI: You've been told she lives in this house?

LOVELACE: Yes, in this area.

AKYEBI: I am afraid there is nobody here by that description.
But if I may ask, what do you want her for?

LOVELACE: Oh well . . . it is nothing difficult. I saw her at work,
you know. And asked about her from another girl who works
with her.

KYEBI: What about her?

LOVELACE: Oh, you know . . . the usual things. I hear she wants
a new job. And . . . there is a place vacant at a factory. So
I thought I could be of help . . .

KYEBI: Is that all?

LOVELACE: (*Snappy*) That's all.

KYEBI: I want a job, anyway, so please come in.

fx: Door closes – kill street noise

LOVELACE: It is easy. I could put you through. If you want it.

KYEBI: I am looking for a job urgently. Please sit down. I'm
afraid the chair is hard and unsafe.

LOVELACE: This is a new place you've moved into?

AKYEBI: Haven't been here for too long.

LOVELACE: The other inmates have gone to work?

AKYEBI: Which other inmates? They are next door.

LOVELACE: Your hus . . . fam . . . (*Trying to look behind or over the screen*)

AKYEBI: I do not share this room with anyone. As you can see, I have little furniture or cooking utensils.

LOVELACE: H*ee* . . . I see. So you don't have to cook for anyone?

AKYEBI: I tell you, I live here alone.

LOVELACE: You can do the work then. Lovelace Smart is the name. You can do the work.

AKYEBI: But I have been working at the bar.

LOVELACE: Which bar?

AKYEBI: Ahope Bar.

LOVELACE: Must be you I am looking for. Oh my . . . You must have been there for only two months?

AKYEBI: So you still haven't recognized me? B?

LOVELACE: My . . . how could I fail to recognize you? Must be your cloth. You look different when you wear your uniform.

AKYEBI: If you can help me get this job as you say, I shall be grateful to you.

LOVELACE: Sure, you'll have it.

POLICEMAN: (*Off mic*) Agoo!

fx: Knocking

AKYEBI: (*Going off mic*) Excuse me. (*Off mic*) Yees!

fx: Door opens

What can I do for you?

POLICEMAN: I am a policeman.

AKYEBI: Yes. What is the matter?

POLICEMAN: You don't want the whole world to see a policema questioning you, do you?

AKYEBI: Well, come in, but do what you must do quickly.

LOVELACE: (*Going off mic*) I'll let you know how far I get with the job. See you. Bye bye.

AKYEBI: Bye bye. Mr Policeman, what do you want?

POLICEMAN: You work at Kofi Brokeman's Ahope Bar, don't you?

AKYEBI: Yes, I do.

POLICEMAN: Perhaps you can help me.

AKYEBI: Help you with what? As for me, I can't help any police . . .

POLICEMAN: You've heard we have been rounding up hotel girls.

AKYEBI: Hotel girls?

POLICEMAN: Night-club girls. We are trying to stop them from selling their thing for money.

AKYEBI: Oh, I see. I was scared, you know. I thought . . .

POLICEMAN: They and those crooks, the men who 'protect' them and get them customers, what do they call them?

AKYEBI: Pilots!

POLICEMAN: Yes, now how did you know, I wonder? Well, we are arresting them.

AKYEBI: This has nothing to do with me, has it?

POLICEMAN: It has, or it might – now or soon.

AKYEBI: How?

POLICEMAN: At least, the women are a disgrace to Ghanaian womanhood.

AKYEBI: Then the men are also a disgrace to Ghanaian manhood?

POLICEMAN: They are men.

AKYEBI: What do you mean?

POLICEMAN: Moreover they are there because of the women, to protect them, apart from finding men who want to buy their thing.

AKYEBI: Papa Polisi, please, I don't think I should bother my head over what other people want to do with their lives. I am afraid I can't help you, so please look on your way.

POLICEMAN: I think you can. That's why I came to you.

AKYEBI: Tell you what? Let your Government pass a decree saying that any man caught buying . . . you know . . . from any such woman will be sent to Preventive Detention.

POLICEMAN: Listen to that! And she says she can't help me. I haven't met many women who are pretty as well as intelligent . . . like you. (*Pause*) Yes . . . what else shall I tell the Government?

AKYEBI: Oh yes, I mean it. If you men do not ask, there would be nobody to sell to.

POLICEMAN: I agree with you.

AKYEBI: And stop arresting them. Simply arresting them.

POLICEMAN: It is not just arresting them. We fine them. Those
who are not able to pay the fine, we lock them up.

AKYEBI: But they come out again, after some time.

POLICEMAN: Well . . .

AKYEBI: And those who pay the fine get away . . . probably to
go back to the same life.

POLICEMAN: Woman, you should be doing some other job than
serving at a beer bar. How far did you go at school?

AKYEBI: Not far.

POLICEMAN: How far?

AKYEBI: Not far enough to get me a job in an office. And I have
no money to trade with.

POLICEMAN: But meanwhile you are doing this job as a bar girl,
which isn't bad. Or is it?

AKYEBI: Well . . . how-for-do!

POLICEMAN: But these other women do not want to work.

AKYEBI: Don't they? How do they get food to eat? Where do
they get all the expensive dresses, shoes, handbags, and the
large multicoloured ear-rings and bangles?

POLICEMAN: You are right. I will say they make so much money
you have no idea.

AKYEBI: I am afraid I must hurry to work. I had a lot of
difficulty before I got this job at the bar, I wouldn't like to
be late. (*Going off mic*) Sorry I couldn't be of help to you.

fx: Door opens; street noises

POLICEMAN: Well, I'll be back. (*Going off mic*) From now on, we
are friends. Bye bye. (*Makes loud, sucking noise*)

AKYEBI: Let go she – did you see that. He shook hands, then he
licked his fingers. What is this I am going to live with? Hm.
I come from my village to town to work. The first man I
meet starts pushing ten cedis into my palm. Now another man
comes along and he seems to want an unmarried woman for
a wife. Well, I say to myself, marriage or a regular job, I
must get one or the other. What happens next? The
advertisement changes from marriage to an offer of a job. I
like it, I say. And now this 'Koti' also comes and what does
he say? He is arresting women who sell their bodies. And
some of the men who encourage the women. But he leaves
untouched some of these same men who encourage the
women. Eh, I must get ready for work, where is my uniform

This work is hard, oh really I look forward to sleeping. Tell me, what does the policeman mean by shaking hands with me and licking his fingers?

Fade out

Fade in

fx: Knocking. Cock crowing

PAMONIE: (*Off mic*) Agoo Akyebi. It's me, Pamonie. I am here as I said I would be.

fx: Bed creaks

AKYEBI: (*Going off mic sleepily.*) Please – one moment – oh, is it morning already?

fx: Door opens

PAMONIE: (*Off mic*) Good morning, my dear. Just from sleep, I see.

fx: A kiss, followed by noise of men carrying in furniture

PAMONIE: (*Coming in on mic*) There – now don't worry at all. My men won't be long. There, don't keep the lady waiting – the rug there, coffee table here, chairs there, there and there.

AKYEBI: Am I dreaming?

PAMONIE: When I heard you were unmarried and working at Ahope Bar, I knew you would need some furniture, so – thank you, men – here you are – now off you go.

MEN: (*Murmur*) Thanks.

fx: Door closes

PAMONIE: And here's a small present.

AKYEBI: A parcel!

PAMONIE: Go on – unwrap it.

fx: Unwrapping of paper

AKYEBI: Oh, a nightdress – how lovely.

PAMONIE: Go on.

AKYEBI: And a – a man's cloth. Oh they are pretty! Sprayed furniture, an armchair, pouf, and rug. Oh, thaaank you ve-e-ery much. This is just like the Mistress's room I used to sweep when I was in the Girl's Boarding School. I used to dream, often, that one day I would pass Middle Form 4, go to a Commercial School and probably be a secretary one day. Then I would have a room like this, beautiful high-heeled shoes and . . . hmm. Then (*Pause*) I had to leave school because my mother said she had no money to pay my fees.

PAMONIE: Has your mother many children?

AKYEBI: I am the only one.

PAMONIE: And she made you leave school!

AKYEBI: I am not sure of exactly what happened to Mama. She's been saying she was forced to pawn her jewellery, but still – something about a lover – if mother could have such a thing.

PAMONIE: Well . . . you have your nice room now.

AKYEBI: Thanks to you. (*Pause*) May I ask you something?

PAMONIE: Do, pretty one.

AKYEBI: (*Shyly*) Oh. (*Pause*) Why are you so kind to me?

PAMONIE: I like you.

AKYEBI: Why do you like me?

PAMONIE: You attract me.

AKYEBI: How?

PAMONIE: You look like someone who could be kind to me.

AKYEBI: I can't think of any way in which I could be kind to you.

PAMONIE: Who knows! (*Pause*)

AKYEBI: I'll get you something to eat.

PAMONIE: Thanks. I just had breakfast at the Hotel Transcontinental.

AKYEBI: Ei, there. (*Pause*) I'll tidy up my bed.

PAMONIE: Sit down.

AKYEBI: Let me change into . . .

PAMONIE: Come here. Sit and talk to me while I smoke my pipe.

(*Pause. Pamonie puffs at his pipe*)

AKYEBI: You are looking through me.

Pause

PAMONIE: Seems I have seen this face, your face, somewhere. Must be a long time, I can't place it.

AKYEBI: You have travelled much?

PAMONIE: Much. Before I got settled, I used to travel from village to village selling drugs.

AKYEBI: Are you a pharmacist, then?

PAMONIE: Never been. But I could give injections. In those days the villagers would buy three leaves of toilet paper for one shilling and sixpence – fifteen new pesewas.

AKYEBI: Why?

PAMONIE: A cure for piles! (*Both burst out laughing*) And since I travelled outside the country, I was able to do some work for Lebanese smugglers. I only had to decide to make a village my base for a month or two and a landlord would offer me a room free. I had women who were supposed to be wives at almost every base. Temporary, mind you, but one or two were loyal . . . and useful.

AKYEBI: When was all this?

PAMONIE: Oh . . . ten, eight, six years . . . until recently. Of course, I've changed completely now. About three years ago, when I had enough money to start my new business, I shook everything off, hawking, smuggling, women and all.

AKYEBI: All the women? To the last one?

PAMONIE: I still have one . . . you!

AKYEBI: You'll take me to your house to see it?

PAMONIE: Go and get dressed and tidy up your room. You'll take this musical box this evening. You see it plays when you open it, see.

fx: Musical box plays

PAMONIE: A Lebanese driving a sports car will collect it from you. (*Going off mic*) Anything you want, you only have to ask me. See you tonight. Bye bye.

fx: Door opens – low street noises

AKYEBI: Bye bye. These expensive presents I am taking. So he tells me when to dress, when to tidy up my room. Where is my brush, I wonder? Am I going to have the freedom to do just what I want to do? Say, go to dances, visit friends? Elderly ones, what would you advise me to do?

LOVELACE: (*Off mic, whistling a pop song*)

AKYEBI: Who is that – eh, Lovelace. Well, my room is tidy – but perhaps I'd better hide Pamonie's cloth before he comes in.

LOVELACE: (*From off mic*) Baby!

fx: Noises of cloth being hidden

LOVELACE: (*Off mic*) Alomo! (*Stops on seeing the change*)

fx: Door shuts – kill street noises

AKYEBI: Please don't stand there surprised, come in – have I been offered the job?

LOVELACE: (*Coming on mic*) Hi baby! What is this transformation of your room?

AKYEBI: Oh . . . eh . . . (*Lying*) My uncle packed them in.

LOVELACE: He must adore you.

AKYEBI: Yes – please sit – my uncle is – er – he is going back to school. What about the job? Did they tell you when I should start? I'll want to give my manager notice.

LOVELACE: It won't be long. I'll let you know as soon as they give the go.

AKYEBI: You'll find me at the bar.

LOVELACE: I don't mind coming all the way here.

AKYEBI: Most of the time I am at the bar. (*Pause*)

LOVELACE: I thought you might need these for the new work. A parcel.

fx: Wrapping paper rustles

AKYEBI: What nice paper, and inside, what a pretty bag!

LOVELACE: For work.

AKYEBI: What a shape!

LOVELACE: Polygon, see?

AKYEBI: The colour is not common in these parts.

LOVELACE: Magenta, that's what they call this colour!

AKYEBI: Oh. (*She kisses it. Pause*) During my confirmation all the girls except me carried handbags.

LOVELACE: Look inside.

fx: Rustle as scarf pulled out

AKYEBI: Be-au-ti-ful!

LOVELACE: To cover your hair. To protect it against the chemicals. All the girls do.

AKYEBI: You've been inside the factory?

LOVELACE: I work there . . . the bag is big enough to contain packed lunch for two, isn't it?

AKYEBI: Must be. (*Pause*) But I wish I could keep both bag and scarf for special occasions.

LOVELACE: Tell you what. I'll get coloured bulbs . . . Blue? . . .

Red? . . . creates a cosy atmosphere in the evenings. We'll celebrate the furnishings this weekend. It's going to be bourgeois!

AKYEBI: And quiet . . . yes. (*Softly*) My landlord. He is fussy about noise and visitors.

LOVELACE: He gets his rent.

AKYEBI: Ssh . . . my uncle's instructions. They are friends.

LOVELACE: Forget about him. Baby, come here!

AKYEBI: Eh – ha ha – don't squeeze so hard – oh!

POLICEMAN: (*Off mic*) Agoo! Is there no-one in there?

AKYEBI: Eh. Must be my uncle.

LOVELACE: Hum, wait a moment – that's better – now let him come. I am helping to find you a job, remember.

AKYEBI: Or . . . the landlord? The voice.

POLICEMAN: (*Off mic*) Excuse me . . . it is the police.

AKYEBI: That policeman again! (*Pause*) Please get in there.

LOVELACE: What is this? Do I need to hide?

AKYEBI: Who knows? It may be you he is tracking.

LOVELACE: (*Resisting, but going off mic*) I have a clean record.

AKYEBI: Er . . . well . . . he may be coming after me. In there. We may have some fun. (*Going off mic*) Hurry, under the bed quick!

fx: Door opens

AKYEBI: (*Off mic*) Oh, it's you.

POLICEMAN: (*Coming on mic*) Didn't I hear voices in here?

AKYEBI: I was singing in the back there.

POLICEMAN: Hm – I see. That bag is really pretty.

AKYEBI: Won't you sit down?

POLICEMAN: This place looks different. Cosy, eh?

AKYEBI: Thank you, but I'm sure you didn't come to see whether I'm cosy or not. What can I do for you?

POLICEMAN: Just looking around – mm – a thick rug – oh, by the way, someone carried your suggestion a step further.

AKYEBI: My suggestion?

POLICEMAN: In the papers.

fx: Rustle of newspaper opening

POLICEMAN: A reader suggests that the Government should legalize prostitution.

AKYEBI: I do not understand.

POLICEMAN: That the Government should allow prostitution.

fx: Newspaper rustling

AKYEBI: Let me see. What's that? A picture of . . . a big raid at 'Christmas in Bethlehem', 'Twilight', 'Anidaso', 'Blue Sky', 'Slim Staff', 'Crimson' . . . and 'Ahope'! When was this?

POLICEMAN: Early this morning, after your shift had left.

AKYEBI: (*Alarmed*) Is that why you come here?

POLICEMAN: No. Mind if I sit down?

AKYEBI: Oh! (*Sighing*)

POLICEMAN: What's that?

AKYEBI: Oh, it is a musical box my uncle gave me to deliver to his friend.

POLICEMAN: (*Picks up box*) Some women cover up their husbands and boy friends even though they are aware that the men are smugglers, gamblers and even burglars. Would you encourage your husband if you found him guilty of any of these?

AKYEBI: Papa Polisi, you must have learnt enough about me to know that the last thing I shall want to do is get the law against me.

fx: Musical box opens and plays

POLICEMAN: You know, these are very popular with Lebanese.

AKYEBI: No, I didn't know.

fx: Alarm bell of a clock

AKYEBI: (*Going off mic*) I must be getting ready to go to work.

POLICEMAN: Of course – you always are. I'll see you at work. (*Going off mic*) It's a nice box. Bye bye.

fx: Door closes

AKYEBI: (*Giggles*) Sorry, dear, let's continue.

LOVELACE: (*Coming in on mic*) My . . . haven't you dismissed him? Come on then, in here. (*Both giggle*)

fx: Fade out on giggles and musical box

fx: Street noises fade in

AKYE: (*Coming in on mic*) Heirs of this town, I am B's mother. She is my only child and I simply adore her. I brought her

up in the best way I knew, except that something, some
devil crossed my way, preventing me from seeing her through
Standard Seven (*pronounced Sana seben*). All the same, I trained
her well at home. I made her sweep the house, fetch water
from the riverside, and work on the farm. I taught her to
keep her clothing neat. I had her confirmed in church. Few
mothers are as affectionate to their children as I am to my B.
(*Going off mic*) Agoo B! My B!

AKYEBI: (*Off mic*) Who could that be?

fx: Door opens

Ma! You look healthy. Welcome.

fx: As door closes, cut street noises

AKYE: (*Looking around*) Hmm, you've bought a lot of things in a
short time.

AKYEBI: It's been hard work. Here, Mother, this is a comfortable
chair.

AKYE: I hear so. You are not spending all your money on finery,
are you?

AKYEBI: I am saving so that I can pay to learn dressmaking.
(*Pause*) Ma, may I ask what brought you here this hot
afternoon?

AKYE: You didn't go to work today?

AKYEBI: We run shifts. I'll go in the late afternoon.

AKYE: All right. I have been receiving the fish, provisions, and
the cloth. The money too. All the things you've been sending.
People tell me you are getting on well, but I said I must
come and see with my own eyes. Some girls come here, they
tell their people, to work, but they are seen very often at
beer bars and hotels. They don't do any work. I know I have
brought you up well, you will do no such thing.

AKYEBI: Ma, my office is at Burma Camp.

AKYE: Ei! The big soldiers' place? I'm glad, even though my
daughter has no Standard Seven Certificate (*She pronounces it
– Sana Seben Sefitikate*) she has enough of good home training
for anybody to give her work. Er . . . B . . . You know it was
my greatest wish to send you to school as far as you could go.
But . . .

AKYEBI: Ma, you said you hadn't money.

AKYE: Well, not quite that. Now that you have a job and are

grown, I'd better tell you, in plain language . . . that men
are not good. I met a doctor (*Pronounced doketa*) during one of
my trading expeditions. He was good to me at the beginning,
I must say. So I put all my trust in him.

AKYEBI: But Ma, what has this got to do with my schooling?

AKYE: You let me tell you . . . the reason why I couldn't pay
your fees. He talked me into believing that he made a lot of
money selling medicine. Not only that. He persuaded me to
pawn my necklace, a big one your father gave me when we
first married, then there were 'Bota' beads, and about three
big 'Mpow' – B, you mustn't put red paint on your nails!
Get a blade and scrape it off . . . quick.

fx: Noise of B going off mic and returning – noise of scraping

Hm. Later I learnt the doctor himself gave the man who
bought my jewels the money to pay for them. I remember he
offered a low price. I tell you, if a man starts being too kind
to you, look out, he may be making some use of you. The
doctor vanished from my life!

AKYEBI: Didn't you get the police to arrest him?

AKYE: Perhaps one day, but not then. (*Pause*) Er . . . I see you
are happy but I have some good plan for you. It should suit
you.

AKYEBI: If my tastes haven't changed.

AKYE: Not in marriage affairs. Teacher Asoko. You know him,
don't you? He wants to marry you.

AKYEBI: But the vocation school . . .

AKYE: Don't argue with your mother. I am your mother. It is
out of struggling that I brought you up, after your father
deserted us.

AKYEBI: I am going to learn dressmaking. But they will also
teach me to read and write.

AKYE: Teacher Asoko is all ready . . . to marry you. *He*, he has
bought an Air Tight, (*Which she pronounces Ea Tart; she is
referring to a Trunk*) a number of dumaso cloth, toilet things,
perfume . . . even pots and pans. As for reading and writing,
he can teach you better.

AKYEBI: Don't you think I shall be happier when I marry, if I
have learnt some profession? Then I won't have to depend
on my husband all the time. I can still buy your needs from
my own pocket.

AKYE: You can still make money. Bake bread, prepare kenkey. That's what most teachers' wives do.

AKYEBI: Ma, give me time to think of it, to consider certain things.

AKYE: Think of it. (*Pause*) B., it's not good keeping your hair so unkempt. All the long heavy hair I used to spend hours plaiting nicely, you have burnt it all with hot comb!

AKYEBI: I shall comb it before I go to work.

AKYE: Tie a headkerchief. It's nicer.

fx: Noise of fumbling with shoes

AKYEBI: I'll see you, Ma. I have to go to the shop to buy cosmetics.

AKYE: Not on those stilts. Haven't you any sandals with flat soles? You can wear these pretty high-heeled shoes to church.

AKYEBI: (*Protesting, going off mic*) My manager insists that we should appear pretty in the office. Bye.

fx: Door opens and closes

AKYE: Hm! (*Short humming sound*) (*Moves round mic during speech*) I wonder how much money has gone into the buying of all these things. Look at some bag. Ei, there is scarf in it. This beautiful blanket that she walks on: she could have covered the floor with ordinary mat. All the money she must have paid for this, I could trade with it. Aa . . . well, she is lucky. Has always been lucky. Look at where some of the things lie hidden. What is that? A . . . dress. A dance dress or a wedding dress? What is man's cloth doing in this room? I hope it is not a man who is buying all these things for her. (*Pause*) Of course, if she works in the Government's office, she certainly receives big pay. So she can afford anything. She has been lucky though . . . getting a good job . . . and she not having any paper . . . certificate (*She says setikate . . . sefitikate*) or what? Amma Ntoa's daughter is still at home. She said she has paper. Today she wears that 'piaans' which simply doesn't permit her to walk properly. Another day she says she is wearing a dress, but her whole bottom is in the sun. Tweaa! and these call themselves ladies. They should come and see my daughter. She has also become something.

fx: Suddenly loud highlife music

AKYE: Ei, modern big town life. How people live in this noise
everywhere, I don't know. (*Pause*) I'll just stay for some
three days and . . . Oya . . . back to my village.

fx: Door opens

AKYE: Ei, somebody has come into the house!
POLICEMAN: (*Off mic*) Is anybody at home?

fx: Door closes

AKYE: You want my daughter, I think?
POLICEMAN: (*Coming in on mic*) Oh, you are her mother?
AKYE: You have come to see her?
POLICEMAN: Sort of . . . yes . . . but it doesn't matter if she is
not at home.
AKYE: Hm . . . do you know my daughter very well?
POLICEMAN: Oh yes. I have been taking care of her. This is a
bad city you know.
AKYE: What do you want to tell her when she comes?
POLICEMAN: Oh . . . just that, I had to find out how she was
getting on in her job, I am trying to get a better job for her.
AKYE: Ei, no. She doesn't want to give up the present job. It is a
good one.
POLICEMAN: (*Cautious*) She has told you about it?
AKYE: Yes . . . yes. She likes it. I would insist that she keeps it.
Working with white people and big Ghanaians . . . it's no
child's play working in Burma Camp . . . the Government
office, you know.
POLICEMAN: I thought her job was too demanding, that's why I
thought she was trying to get a new one. But I think you are
right. It is nicer where she works.
AKYE: Is it true? She says her manager insists that they wear
high heels and nice clothes to work.
POLICEMAN: That's right. Public relations.
AKYE: I hear people of all sorts call in there.
POLICEMAN: Public Relations, that's her job. And the people are
big ones. But this is what I'm interested in, her music box,
I've been keeping my eye on it. Don't you think it's a bit
heavy for a music box?
AKYE: Ahh. I . . .
POLICEMAN: It's all right, I didn't expect you to know. But
these boxes can hold music . . .

fx: Music box clicks open and plays

POLICEMAN: . . . and other things. I'm sure B. won't mind if I borrow it.

fx: Box clicks shut and music stops

But really she is lucky to have a nice place like this.

fx: Knocking on door

PAMONIE: (*Off mic*) It's me, your Pamonie.
AKYE: Ame.

fx: Door opens

PAMONIE: (*Off mic*) Is B. in?
AKYE: No, B. has gone to work. Would you like to wait for her? I don't think she will be back soon, though. I am her mother.
PAMONIE: (*Coming in on mic*) I see. Well, I shall wait for her. I must see her. It is very important.
POLICEMAN: Well . . . mother, I must be going now. (*Going off mic*) I shall see you again soon. And please tell B. I was here.
AKYE: (*Going off mic*) All right; but let me see the back of your head.

fx: Door closes

(*Coming on mic*) Oh, Owura, I am sorry I left you alone in the darkness. Let me put on the light . . . I wonder, where is the switch.

PAMONIE: Oh, don't worry, I know where it is. I'll put it on myself.

fx: Light switch click

PAMONIE: Who are you?
AKYE: Pamonie! Pamonie! Is that what you call yourself now? What are you doing here?
PAMONIE: And what are you doing in my girl's room?
AKYE: Your girl – this is my daughter's room!
PAMONIE: Your daughter! That explains it. I told B. I had seen her face somewhere.
AKYE: Just this afternoon I was telling B. how I gave my whole capital to you – pawned my valuables and gave everything to you. You duped me!
PAMONIE: I didn't mean to.

AKYE: Why then did you vanish from my life?

PAMONIE: I didn't mean to, I say.

AKYE: Didn't you?

PAMONIE: The police were after me.

AKYE: I see them after you.

PAMONIE: No, I was a wanted man.

AKYE: I also told them you had been smuggling and registering injection without licence. And now you are after my daughter too.

PAMONIE: I'll pay you back.

AKYE: It is late . . . you made my head hit the ground. It's late. B. had to leave school.

PAMONIE: What should I do?

AKYE: I'll sue you. I shall let them put you inside.

PAMONIE: I'm married with children. Don't do that to me.

AKYE: I'll report you to the police, tell them I have found you.

AKYEBI: (*Off mic*) No, you mustn't come in with me. My mother has just arrived from the village.

LOVELACE: (*Off mic*) No fear, baby, she'll have gone to see the neighbours.

PAMONIE: My B. – a man!

AKYEBI: Later, when she's gone. Until then, no fear!

AKYE: What's this?

LOVELACE: O.K. You win, no fun – business.

AKYEBI: You do not want my people to know you? Or, do you? Don't bring yourself.

LOVELACE: Oh. Jokes apart, you said you want to go to a vocational school and now I have some entry forms . . . all you do is fill them in and give them to me with the registration fee. Now what is all this woman do?

AKYEBI: Forms, have you really got forms for me? As for that then . . .

LOVELACE: Look at her, 'As for that' what?

AKYEBI: You may come in then.

LOVELACE: A kiss first, mind you . . .

fx: Door opens

AKYEBI: (*Squeals*)

LOVELACE: Oh, I see . . . there are . . . (*Pulls himself together*) (*Coming in on mic*) B.'s mother I guess. Welcome, Ma. And this gent?

PAMONIE: I am Pamonie. And who are you?

LOVELACE: I am B.'s friend and I hope to –

PAMONIE: You have hit madness. You small boy!

LOVELACE: Why are you so hot, are you going to marry your niece yourself?

PAMONIE: Go! Out of this house.

fx: Scuffle

AKYEBI: Oh no! Oh no! Nobody is going to fight here. I will not be here.

AKYE: Trouble has come.

fx: Policemen's whistle off mic

POLICEMAN: (*Off mic*) You, constable, cover the rear of the premises. You, Constable Issa, follow me.

CONSTABLES: (*Off mic*) Sah.

POLICEMAN: Come on.

AKYEBI: Ehee! It is the police who are coming to take you away. Fight on, I am gone.

fx: Scuffles

ISSA: No sir, madam. I catch you proper this time, you no fit run away. You no be fit. No be so, Corporal.

POLICEMAN: You are right, Issa. She won't run away, so you need not hold her. Everybody should stay where they are, the house is surrounded. Issa, that man, the one they call Pamonie, hold him.

fx: Scuffle

POLICEMAN: I have a warrant for the arrest of the man currently going under the assumed name of Pamonie on charges of diamond smuggling. As evidence I hold a music box containing a collection of diamonds concealed in a secret drawer. It is the prosecution's case that Pamonie intended to pass these diamonds to certain Lebanese who frequent the Ahope Bar. To this end he inveigled his way into the life of Miss Akyebi, a . . . very attractive girl . . . who, partly due to the inadequacy of her mother, was dangerously exposed in the city and, had not the police been up to the mark, might have fallen into the clutches of unscrupulous exploiters like the notorious confidence trickster Lovelace Smart – Yes, hold him too, constable. I expect we can pin something on him at the station.

LOVELACE: Take your dirty hands off me! You bugu-bugu police. Now, where is the warrant for my arrest?

POLICEMAN: Hold him, constable.

ISSA: I fit, Sah.

AKYE: My daughter. What is this? If I haven't seen my daughter for a long time, and I am now coming to spend three days with her, what is this I am going to see? Buee!! I hit my head!

LOVELACE: Steady. No bullying, no pushing about, no beating, and no accidentally falling downstairs at the police station. I refuse to allow myself to be arrested. Here is my student identity card with my address. When you are sure you have found, or manufactured, evidence against me, then pick me. Or else get ready to tell me why I shouldn't sue you for defamation of character.

AKYEBI: Papa Polisi, I tell you I know nothing about diamonds. If I see diamonds I will not know. Ask Pamonie if he has shown anything to me?

PAMONIE: Corporal, I have given these women enough trouble. Akyebi has only been my 'pretty little good girl'. She knew nothing of the diamonds.

POLICEMAN: If you think that kind speech will do you any good in Court you are mistaken. We have no charge against B. We will only call her as a witness against you.

AKYEBI: O, my bad head that I carry everywhere. Just when I got these forms and hope to learn some trade.

AKYE: The deer who conceived and delivered her child did not get cloth to wear. How can you, the baby deer, find cloth? Nananom, eat this my case for me. My daughter has seen disgrace.

POLICEMAN: (*Going off mic*) Come on Pamonie, Lovelace. Bring them, Issa.

ISSA: Sah! Make you come go.

LOVELACE: B. has done nothing. She is going to Awura Abena's vocational school to learn dressmaking –

AKYE: But this witnessing, she is going to stand in the box to do . . . who wants a woman . . .

LOVELACE: (*Going off mic*) There's no rush! – and cooking, and

I am going to marry her. Love does not know the crooked pelvis. B., fill the forms and post them.

fx: Footsteps, protestations, commands going off mic – door shuts

AKYE: (*Pause*) B., so he is going to marry you? What are you going to do in that school then?

AKYEBI: Ma, he hasn't asked you for me yet. Wait until you drink my head drink. Men and women of this town, do we make one mind?

fx: Highlife music under

When I arrived in this town I had neither job nor man. Those orphans among you, this is like passing behind some house. You hear a mother advising her child. And you also listen. As it is, if red doesn't win, black will. I am going to learn. When I am sitting behind my sewing-machine, or standing in front of my fire brewing soup – let any cheat of a man come to make me into a company pot!

fx: Bring up music to end